Math Tutor:
Pre-Algebra Skills

Author: Hal Torrance

Editors: Mary Dieterich and Sarah M. Anderson

Proofreader: Margaret Brown

COPYRIGHT © 2011 Mark Twain Media, Inc.

ISBN 978-1-58037-577-1

Printing No. CD-404145

Mark Twain Media, Inc., Publishers
Distributed by Carson-Dellosa Publishing LLC

Table of Contents

ii

How to Use This Book

Each new concept is introduced in a short **Absorb** section. The Absorb section primarily focuses on a single skill or concept. Key terms are highlighted for easy identification. The **Apply** section then gives the student practice in that skill. Each concept is followed by **Extra Practice** pages to give students opportunities for further reinforcement of the skills learned.

Pre-algebra is considered to be something of a terminal arithmetic course. What this means for the student is that pre-algebra is a course that links many topics together before the student proceeds to more abstract mathematics courses.

Since pre-algebra is largely arithmetic-based, mastery of arithmetic becomes an important aspect of the pre-algebra curriculum. A student who does not understand basic topics, such as factoring a number or adding two fractions, for instance, will have little success once these concepts are framed around far more abstract variables. Pre-algebra becomes an important transition course not so much for the portion of it that is new to the students but for the larger portion that should already be familiar.

This book has been arranged in a systematic way, keeping the sequential nature of mathematics in mind. However, sections may be used in any order that best fits the particular needs of the student, even if that means skipping around a bit.

The section **Final Review: All Topics** can serve as a good pretest if one is needed for planning a more focused course of study. There are also two **Section Reviews** that focus on cumulative skills presented to that point in the book.

What follows are descriptions and suggested uses for each section of this book.

1. **Factoring Numbers:** reviews factors, an underlying concept in reducing fractions and composite numbers.

2. **Adding and Subtracting Fractions:** includes problems with both like and unlike denominators and problems with mixed numbers. A quick review of reducing fractions is included as a starter activity.

3. **Multiplying and Dividing Fractions:** includes problems with both simple fractions and mixed numbers. A quick review of improper fractions is included as a starter activity.

4. **Positive and Negative Numbers:** reviews the concept of negative numbers with practice adding and subtracting negatives. Problems involving fractions are included.

5. **Multiplying and Dividing With Negative Numbers:** reviews rules for multiplying and dividing negative numbers. Problems involving fractions are also included.

How to Use This Book (cont.)

6. **Order of Operations:** reviews symbols and rules used for determining order of operations in evaluating math expressions.

   Section Review 1 and Section Review 1 Extra Practice: provides practice problems for reviewing previous sections.

7. **Squares and Square Roots:** reviews the fundamental exponent [2] and taking a square root. A calculator is recommended for this activity.

8. **Exponents:** reviews base numbers and exponents. A calculator may be used for this activity.

9. **What Is a Variable?:** reviews basic use of variables in mathematics.

10. **Expressions With Variables:** provides practice evaluating expressions with variable values provided and for solving simple equations by inspection.

11. **More Practice With Variables:** combining like terms is reviewed as a method for simplifying expressions.

    Section Review 2 and Section Review 2 Extra Practice: provides practice problems for reviewing previous sections.

12. **Perimeter and Area:** reviews the concepts of perimeter and area. This section links the process of finding perimeter and area to solving expressions with variables.

13. **Volume:** reviews the concept of volume with emphasis on solving expressions with variables.

14. **Working With Circles:** reviews formulas for finding circumference and area of circles. A calculator is recommended for this section.

15. **Basic Properties of Numbers:** reviews basic number properties with applicable examples.

16. **Studying Data:** reviews basic measures of data including median, mode, and mean. A calculator is recommended for this activity.

17. **Word Problem Workshop:** reviews various topics covered in previous sections through the use of applied word problems. A calculator may be used for this activity.

    Final Review: All Sections and **Final Review Extra Practice** provide practice problems for reviewing all sections. Due to the length, the Final Review should be split into two different sessions for students. A calculator is recommended for some exercises. An alternative use for this section would be as a pretest to define areas that need additional attention before beginning the activities in this book.

Name: _____   Date: _____

Section **1** Factoring Numbers

ABSORB

These are the **factors** of 16: 1, 2, 4, 8, 16. This is because 1 x 16 = 16, 2 x 8 = 16, and 4 x 4 = 16.

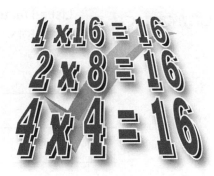

A **composite number**, such as 16, can possibly be reduced if it appears in a fraction or equation. A **prime number** has only 1 and itself as factors and, therefore, cannot be reduced. The numbers 11, 13, and 17 are a few examples of the many prime numbers. Being able to recognize composite or prime numbers is useful, not only for working with fractions, but also in later applications involving equations.

APPLY

List all factors for each number. Write "prime" if the number has only 1 and itself as factors.

1. 4 _____

2. 12 _____

3. 18 _____

4. 31 _____

5. 48 _____

6. 55 _____

7. 67 _____

8. 71 _____

9. 90 _____

10. 105 _____

11. 111 _____

12. 200 _____

13. 301 _____

14. 400 _____

15. 425 _____

Name: _____ Date: _____

Section 1 Factoring Numbers

EXTRA PRACTICE   List all factors for each number. Write "prime" if the number has only 1 and itself as factors.

1. 5 _____

2. 14 _____

3. 19 _____

4. 32 _____

5. 49 _____

6. 50 _____

7. 68 _____

8. 72 _____

9. 99 _____

10. 110 _____

11. 125 _____

12. 250 _____

13. 305 _____

14. 415 _____

15. 450 _____

16. 500 _____

17. 575 _____

18. 605 _____

19. 620 _____

20. 702 _____

Name: _____ Date: _____

Section ❷ Adding and Subtracting Fractions

ABSORB Adding or subtracting fractions with like denominators is a fairly straightforward process, as shown in the following examples. Only the numerators are added or subtracted. The final step is reducing the answer to lowest terms.

Example 1: $\frac{1}{5} + \frac{2}{5} =$

$$\frac{1}{5} + \frac{2}{5} = \frac{3}{5}$$

Example 2: $\frac{5}{6} - \frac{1}{6} =$

$$\frac{5}{6} - \frac{1}{6} = \frac{4}{6}$$

reduces to $\frac{2}{3}$

Fractions without like denominators must be changed before adding or subtracting can take place. The process is called "finding a **common denominator**." This process is shown in the following examples.

Example 3: $\frac{1}{8} + \frac{2}{3} =$

$$\frac{3}{24} + \frac{16}{24} =$$

$$\frac{3}{24} + \frac{16}{24} = \frac{19}{24}$$

Example 4: $2 - \frac{6}{10} =$

$$1\frac{10}{10} - \frac{6}{10} =$$

$$1\frac{10}{10} - \frac{6}{10} = 1\frac{4}{10}$$

reduces to $1\frac{2}{5}$

APPLY **QUICK REVIEW** Reduce the following fractions to lowest terms.

1. $\frac{6}{10} =$ _____

2. $\frac{10}{110} =$ _____

3. $\frac{9}{45} =$ _____

4. $\frac{2}{50} =$ _____

5. $\frac{7}{28} =$ _____

6. $\frac{15}{18} =$ _____

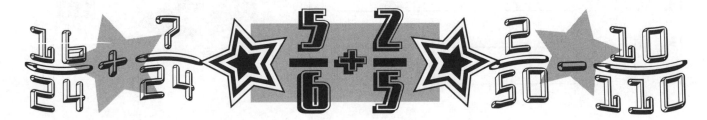

Name:_____ Date:_____

Section **2** Adding and Subtracting Fractions

EXTRA PRACTICE   Reduce the following fractions to lowest terms.

1. $\frac{7}{10}$ = _____

2. $\frac{20}{220}$ = _____

3. $\frac{8}{45}$ = _____

4. $\frac{2}{75}$ = _____

5. $\frac{7}{21}$ = _____

6. $\frac{15}{35}$ = _____

7. $\frac{8}{20}$ = _____

8. $\frac{10}{120}$ = _____

9. $\frac{8}{36}$ = _____

10. $\frac{2}{40}$ = _____

11. $\frac{9}{63}$ = _____

12. $\frac{15}{30}$ = _____

13. $\frac{8}{10}$ = _____

14. $\frac{30}{330}$ = _____

15. $\frac{5}{45}$ = _____

16. $\frac{2}{60}$ = _____

17. $\frac{3}{21}$ = _____

18. $\frac{16}{18}$ = _____

19. $\frac{9}{10}$ = _____

20. $\frac{50}{500}$ = _____

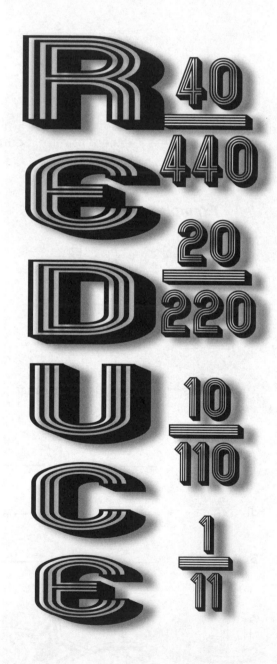

Name: _____ Date: _____

Section **2** Adding and Subtracting Fractions

APPLY Add or subtract as indicated. Some problems will require finding a common denominator. Some problems may require changing a whole number to its fractional equivalent. Reduce answers to lowest terms.

1. $\frac{2}{7} + \frac{3}{7} =$ _____

2. $\frac{8}{24} + \frac{10}{24} =$ _____

3. $\frac{7}{8} - \frac{1}{3} =$ _____

4. $\frac{9}{12} - \frac{6}{36} =$ _____

5. $\frac{4}{5} + \frac{5}{9} =$ _____

6. $\frac{18}{20} - \frac{2}{10} =$ _____

7. $\frac{2}{9} + \frac{2}{81} =$ _____

8. $\frac{10}{15} - \frac{1}{5} =$ _____

9. $1\frac{2}{5} + \frac{4}{5} =$ _____

10. $3 - \frac{6}{8} =$ _____

11. $\frac{4}{22} - \frac{2}{22} =$ _____

12. $\frac{70}{20} - \frac{50}{20} =$ _____

13. $2\frac{6}{8} + \frac{7}{6} =$ _____

14. $\frac{12}{18} + 1\frac{2}{3} =$ _____

15. $2\frac{5}{11} + 3\frac{4}{44} =$ _____

16. $4\frac{2}{3} - 3\frac{2}{6} =$ _____

17. $4\frac{1}{4} - 1\frac{1}{3} =$ _____

18. $2\frac{7}{8} - 1 =$ _____

19. $\frac{55}{8} - 2\frac{4}{16} =$ _____

20. $\frac{22}{10} - 1\frac{1}{5} =$ _____

21. $\frac{1}{8} + 1\frac{1}{4} + \frac{3}{16} =$ _____

22. $2\frac{3}{4} + \frac{20}{5} + 1\frac{5}{20} =$ _____

23. $\frac{2}{5} + 1\frac{4}{6} + \frac{2}{30} =$ _____

24. $\frac{14}{3} + \frac{1}{6} + 2\frac{2}{3} =$ _____

25. $\frac{28}{8} - \left(\frac{1}{8} + \frac{3}{8}\right) =$ _____

Name: _____ Date: _____

Section ② Adding and Subtracting Fractions

EXTRA PRACTICE Add or subtract as indicated. Some problems will require finding a common denominator. Some problems may require changing a whole number to its fractional equivalent. Reduce answers to lowest terms.

1. $\frac{3}{7} + \frac{5}{7} =$ _____

2. $\frac{9}{24} + \frac{12}{24} =$ _____

3. $\frac{6}{8} - \frac{2}{3} =$ _____

4. $\frac{8}{12} - \frac{9}{36} =$ _____

5. $\frac{3}{5} + \frac{6}{9} =$ _____

6. $\frac{19}{20} - \frac{1}{10} =$ _____

7. $\frac{4}{9} + \frac{8}{81} =$ _____

8. $\frac{11}{15} - \frac{1}{9} =$ _____

9. $2\frac{3}{5} + \frac{4}{7} =$ _____

10. $3 - \frac{7}{8} =$ _____

11. $\frac{8}{22} - \frac{6}{22} =$ _____

12. $\frac{80}{20} - \frac{30}{20} =$ _____

13. $\frac{23}{8} + \frac{7}{8} =$ _____

14. $\frac{16}{18} + \frac{6}{3} =$ _____

15. $\frac{28}{11} + \frac{3}{44} =$ _____

16. $\frac{15}{3} - \frac{24}{6} =$ _____

17. $\frac{18}{4} - 1\frac{2}{3} =$ _____

18. $\frac{24}{8} - 2 =$ _____

19. $\frac{56}{8} - \frac{4}{16} =$ _____

20. $\frac{25}{10} - \frac{6}{5} =$ _____

21. $\frac{1}{7} + \frac{5}{4} + \frac{8}{16} =$ _____

22. $\frac{3}{4} + \frac{25}{5} + \frac{5}{20} =$ _____

Section 3 Multiplying and Dividing Fractions

ABSORB

For multiplying fractions, there's no need for a common denominator. The numerator is multiplied by the numerator, and likewise, the denominator is multiplied by the denominator, as shown in the following examples. Keep in mind also that mixed numbers must first be converted to improper fractions. Reducing fractions where possible will also make the process easier.

Example 1: $\frac{4}{6} \times \frac{2}{9} =$

$\frac{2}{3} \times \frac{2}{9} =$

$\frac{2}{3} \times \frac{2}{9} = \frac{4}{27}$

Example 2: $1\frac{1}{6} \times \frac{2}{5} =$

$\frac{7}{6} \times \frac{2}{5} =$

$\frac{7}{6} \times \frac{2}{5} = \frac{14}{30}$

reduces to $\frac{7}{15}$

The main difference in dividing fractions is inverting. **Inverting** is the process of flipping the second fraction so that the division can be performed. (This step actually turns the division problem into a multiplication problem as seen in the following examples.)

Example 3: $\frac{3}{8} \div \frac{1}{2} =$

invert step $\frac{3}{8} \times \frac{2}{1} =$

$\frac{3}{8} \times \frac{2}{1} = \frac{6}{8}$

reduces to $\frac{3}{4}$

Example 4: $1\frac{4}{10} \div \frac{2}{5} =$

$\frac{14}{10} \times \frac{5}{2} =$

can be reduced by cross-dividing $\frac{7}{2} \times \frac{1}{1} =$

$\frac{7}{2} \times \frac{1}{1} = \frac{7}{2}$

reduces to $3\frac{1}{2}$

Name: _____   Date: _____

Section ▶ 3 ▶ Multiplying and Dividing Fractions

APPLY   **QUICK REVIEW**

Convert each mixed number or whole number to its equivalent improper fraction.

1. $3\frac{3}{8}$ = _____

2. $4\frac{5}{8}$ = _____

3. $7\frac{8}{9}$ = _____

4. $1\frac{1}{12}$ = _____

5. 11 = _____

6. $2\frac{4}{15}$ = _____

Multiply or divide as indicated. Reduce answers to lowest terms.

1. $\frac{1}{4} \times \frac{1}{5}$ = _____

2. $\frac{4}{7} \times \frac{8}{16}$ = _____

3. $\frac{6}{15} \times \frac{2}{6}$ = _____

4. $\frac{1}{4} \div \frac{1}{2}$ = _____

5. $\frac{8}{9} \div \frac{1}{3}$ = _____

6. $\frac{2}{10} \div \frac{3}{4}$ = _____

7. $3 \times \frac{1}{4}$ = _____

8. $\frac{20}{8} \times 2$ = _____

9. $2 \div \frac{1}{4}$ = _____

10. $\frac{6}{8} \div 2$ = _____

11. $1\frac{2}{3} \times 4$ = _____

12. $\frac{3}{8} \times 12$ = _____

13. $2\frac{1}{6} \times \frac{4}{9}$ = _____

14. $2\frac{5}{6} \times 1\frac{3}{4}$ = _____

15. $\frac{3}{4} \div 1\frac{1}{2}$ = _____

16. $4\frac{1}{4} \div \frac{1}{8}$ = _____

17. $3\frac{3}{7} \div 1\frac{1}{3}$ = _____

18. $1\frac{4}{9} \div 1\frac{1}{9}$ = _____

19. $1\frac{2}{3} \times \left(\frac{1}{4} \div \frac{3}{8}\right)$ = _____

20. $\left(\frac{3}{8} \times 2\frac{1}{2}\right) \times 4$ = _____

Name: _____ Date: _____

Section ❸ Multiplying and Dividing Fractions

EXTRA PRACTICE Convert each mixed number or whole number to its equivalent improper fraction.

1. $3\frac{3}{5}$ = _____

2. $5\frac{6}{10}$ = _____

3. $6\frac{7}{9}$ = _____

4. $1\frac{4}{12}$ = _____

5. 13 = _____

6. $2\frac{6}{15}$ = _____

7. $4\frac{5}{8}$ = _____

8. $11\frac{3}{4}$ = _____

9. $9\frac{1}{2}$ = _____

10. $2\frac{3}{7}$ = _____

11. 20 = _____

12. $10\frac{2}{3}$ = _____

Convert each improper fraction to its equivalent mixed number or whole number. Reduce answers to lowest terms.

1. $\frac{17}{5}$ = _____

2. $\frac{81}{9}$ = _____

3. $\frac{10}{4}$ = _____

4. $\frac{37}{12}$ = _____

5. $\frac{42}{1}$ = _____

6. $\frac{81}{17}$ = _____

7. $\frac{24}{5}$ = _____

8. $\frac{78}{15}$ = _____

9. $\frac{56}{7}$ = _____

10. $\frac{29}{3}$ = _____

11. $\frac{44}{12}$ = _____

12. $\frac{18}{4}$ = _____

Name: _____ Date: _____

Section 3 Multiplying and Dividing Fractions

EXTRA PRACTICE Multiply or divide as indicated. Reduce answers to lowest terms.

1. $\frac{1}{3} \times \frac{2}{5} =$ _____

2. $\frac{6}{7} \times \frac{9}{18} =$ _____

3. $\frac{7}{15} \times \frac{4}{6} =$ _____

4. $\frac{1}{3} \div \frac{1}{5} =$ _____

5. $\frac{7}{8} \div \frac{2}{3} =$ _____

6. $\frac{1}{5} \div \frac{9}{12} =$ _____

7. $5 \times \frac{6}{8} =$ _____

8. $\frac{15}{7} \times 3 =$ _____

9. $4 \div \frac{2}{3} =$ _____

10. $\frac{9}{8} \div 3 =$ _____

11. $3\frac{3}{4} \times 6 =$ _____

12. $\frac{6}{8} \times 21 =$ _____

13. $2\frac{1}{7} \times \frac{1}{9} =$ _____

14. $2\frac{6}{9} \times 3\frac{7}{8} =$ _____

15. $\frac{4}{5} \div \frac{3}{2} =$ _____

16. $4\frac{2}{8} \div \frac{3}{2} =$ _____

17. $3\frac{4}{7} \div 3\frac{4}{9} =$ _____

18. $\frac{13}{9} \div \frac{10}{9} =$ _____

19. $\frac{5}{3} \times \frac{3}{4} =$ _____

20. $\frac{3}{7} \times \frac{3}{2} =$ _____

21. $2\frac{5}{6} \times \left(\frac{1}{2} \div \frac{2}{3}\right) =$ _____

22. $\left(\frac{6}{7} \times 3\frac{1}{3}\right) \times 2 =$ _____

23. $6 \times \left(\frac{4}{9} \div \frac{5}{7}\right) =$ _____

24. $\left(\frac{3}{4} \times \frac{3}{6}\right) \times 4\frac{4}{5} =$ _____

Section **4** Positive and Negative Numbers

ABSORB   Consider the number line shown below.

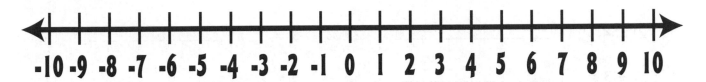

From this number line, we can see that numbers to the left of zero are denoted with a minus sign. **Negative numbers** therefore carry a value of less than zero. **Positive numbers** are placed on the number line to the right of zero and carry a value of more than zero.

One way to think of a negative number is like a hole in the ground that has had dirt removed. The empty hole is like a negative quantity, and a certain amount of dirt would refill that hole. The negative number depicts a quantity that a positive number of like amount would offset. For instance, if 20 shovels of dirt were removed from the hole, it would require 20 shovels of dirt to refill it.

For the solved examples below, try drawing a basic number line on your own paper and counting the quantities as they are added or subtracted.

Example 1: $4 + -4 =$

$4 + -4 = 0$

(Think of this as simply 4 – 4.)

Example 2: $-2 + 5 =$

$-2 + 5 = 3$

(Think of this as simply 5 – 2.)

Example 3: $-4 + -3 =$

$-4 + -3 = -7$

(Think of this as simply 3 + 4, where both quantities are negative.)

Example 4: $1 - -3 =$

$1 - -3 = 4$

(Think of this as simply 1 + 3, since subtracting a negative Is essentially adding a positive.)

Name: _____   Date: _____

Section ④ Positive and Negative Numbers

APPLY   Add or subtract as indicated.

1. 2 + -4 =   _____

2. 3 – -3 =   _____

3. -4 – 3 =   _____

4. -9 – 0 =   _____

5. -3 + -7 =   _____

6. -5 – -7 =   _____

7. -8 + -8 =   _____

8. -6 + 3 =   _____

9. 100 + -2 =   _____

10. 55 – -15 =   _____

11. 0 – 14 =   _____

12. -13 – -20 =   _____

13. 24 – 0 =   _____

14. -8 + -48 =   _____

15. -15 + 5 =   _____

16. -22 + 2 =   _____

17. 500 – -200 =   _____

18. 25 + -50 =   _____

Add or subtract the following fractions. The rules for working with negatives are the same for fractions as for whole numbers. Reduce answers to lowest terms.

19. $2 + -\frac{1}{4} =$ _____

20. $-3 + 3\frac{1}{2} =$ _____

21. $5\frac{1}{2} - -1\frac{1}{2} =$ _____

22. $-\frac{1}{4} - \frac{3}{4} =$ _____

23. $12 - -\frac{3}{4} =$ _____

24. $\frac{2}{3} + -\frac{2}{3} =$ _____

25. $\frac{4}{5} - \frac{5}{4} =$ _____

Name: _____   Date: _____

Section ④ Positive and Negative Numbers

EXTRA PRACTICE   Add or subtract as indicated. Reduce answers to lowest terms, if needed.

1. $3 + -5 =$ _____

2. $5 - -5 =$ _____

3. $-6 - 2 =$ _____

4. $-10 - 0 =$ _____

5. $-6 - -8 =$ _____

6. $-4 - -9 =$ _____

7. $-6 + -6 =$ _____

8. $-3 + 2 =$ _____

9. $200 + -5 =$ _____

10. $35 - -25 =$ _____

11. $0 - 50 =$ _____

12. $-12 - -30 =$ _____

13. $50 - 0 =$ _____

14. $-9 + -68 =$ _____

15. $-10 + 6 =$ _____

16. $-24 + 4 =$ _____

17. $700 - -300 =$ _____

18. $75 + -25 =$ _____

19. $3 + -\frac{1}{3} =$ _____

20. $-5 + 5\frac{1}{5} =$ _____

21. $\frac{7}{8} + -\frac{1}{4} =$ _____

22. $-2\frac{1}{10} - 3\frac{1}{5} =$ _____

23. $5 + -6\frac{4}{9} =$ _____

24. $\frac{1}{2} - \frac{6}{5} =$ _____

25. $-15 + \frac{8}{15} =$ _____

Name: _____   Date: _____

Section **5** Multiplying and Dividing With Negative Numbers

ABSORB

The process of multiplying and dividing negative numbers is made easier by a fixed set of rules. Consider the table below.

> Negative x Negative = Positive
>
> Negative x Positive = Negative
>
> Positive x Negative = Negative
>
> Positive x Positive = Positive
>
> (This table remains the same for division.)

Example 1: $20 \times -4 =$

$20 \times -4 = -80$

Example 2: $-3 \times -12 =$

$-3 \times -12 = 36$

Example 3: $-40 \div 8 =$

$-40 \div 8 = -5$

Example 4: $-9 \times -4 =$

$-9 \times -4 = 36$

APPLY   Multiply or divide as indicated.

1. $12 \times -6 =$ _____

2. $-8 \div 8 =$ _____

3. $-3 \times -3 =$ _____

4. $0 \times -3 =$ _____

5. $45 \times -2 =$ _____

6. $2 \div -1 =$ _____

Name: _____   Date: _____

Section **5** Multiplying and Dividing With Negative Numbers

7. 1 x -9 = _____

8. 30 ÷ -10 = _____

9. -12 x -12 = _____

10. -90 ÷ 9 = _____

11. -2 ÷ -2 = _____

12. 44 x -1 = _____

13. -200 ÷ -20 = _____

14. 24 ÷ -1 = _____

15. -5 x -20 = _____

16. -125 x 4 = _____

17. -200 x -2 = _____

18. -112 x 0 = _____

19. -3 x (4 x -5) = _____

20. 40 x (100 ÷ -10) = _____

Multiply or divide the following fractions. The rules for working with negatives are the same for fractions as for whole numbers. Reduce answers to lowest terms.

21. $-\frac{1}{4}$ x $-\frac{3}{4}$ = _____

22. 5 x $-\frac{4}{5}$ = _____

23. $-\frac{2}{3}$ x $\frac{1}{8}$ = _____

24. -4 ÷ $\frac{1}{4}$ = _____

25. $1\frac{1}{2}$ x -2 = _____

26. $-\frac{5}{6}$ ÷ $\frac{5}{6}$ = _____

27. $-2\frac{1}{2}$ ÷ $-\frac{1}{4}$ = _____

28. $3\frac{3}{4}$ ÷ -3 = _____

29. -2 x $\left(\frac{3}{4} \times \frac{1}{8}\right)$ = _____

30. $4\frac{1}{4}$ x $\left(\frac{7}{8} \div \frac{3}{4}\right)$ = _____

Name: _____   Date: _____

Section ⑤ Multiplying and Dividing With Negative Numbers

EXTRA PRACTICE   Multiply or divide as indicated. Reduce answers to lowest terms if needed.

1. 1 x -20 = _____

2. 25 ÷ -10 = _____

3. -24 x -24 = _____

4. -100 ÷ 10 = _____

5. -3 ÷ -3 = _____

6. 66 x -1 = _____

7. -500 ÷ -50 = _____

8. 12 ÷ -1 = _____

9. -6 x -30 = _____

10. -150 x 5 = _____

11. -300 x -3 = _____

12. -124 x 0 = _____

13. -6 x (8 x -10) = _____

14. 50 x (200 ÷ -10) = _____

15. $-\frac{1}{5}$ x $-\frac{3}{5}$ = _____

16. 6 x $-\frac{7}{8}$ = _____

17. $-\frac{3}{5}$ x $\frac{1}{9}$ = _____

18. -5 ÷ $\frac{1}{5}$ = _____

19. $\frac{3}{2}$ x -6 = _____

20. $-\frac{7}{8}$ ÷ $\frac{7}{8}$ = _____

21. $\frac{3}{10}$ ÷ $-\frac{1}{2}$ = _____

22. $-\frac{4}{9}$ x $\frac{6}{11}$ = _____

23. $-\frac{12}{3}$ ÷ $-\frac{3}{4}$ = _____

24. $-\frac{3}{14}$ x 4 = _____

Section 6 | Order of Operations

ABSORB In working with math expressions, there are certain operations that must be performed first in order for the expression to be correctly evaluated. You've probably seen these basic rules, called the **order of operations**, and used them before.

We know that in a simple math expression, we read through it from left to right, looking for multiplication, division, addition, and subtraction.

Multiplication and/or division operations are performed first (when no other symbols are involved). Then addition and/or subtraction operations are performed.

Example 1:   2 + 3 x 4 =

2 + 12 =

2 + 12 = 14

Example 2:   4 x 3 + 2 x 8 =

12 + 16 =

12 + 16 = 28

Now consider the following symbols: parentheses ( )   brackets [ ]   braces { }

In a math expression, the operations within these symbols are performed in the order shown below:

$$\{ \; [\; (\; \text{first} \;) \; \text{next} \;] \; \text{last} \; \}$$

Begin performing the operations within parentheses, then move to that part inside the brackets, and finally complete that portion within the braces.

Example 3:   (2 + 4 − 1) + (5 x 6) =

(5) + (30) =

5 + 30 = 35

Example 4:   [50 − (2 x 12) + (12 ÷ 2)] =

[50 − 24 + 6] =

26 + 6 =

26 + 6 = 32

$$\{4 \times [\, 6 - 3 + (8 + 3)\,]\} =$$
$$\{4 \times [\, 6 - 3 + 11\,]\} =$$
$$\{4 \times [\, 3 + 11\,]\} =$$
$$\{4 \times 14\} =$$
$$56$$

Name: _____ Date: _____

Section **6** Order of Operations

APPLY   Solve the expressions using order of operations rules.

1. 7 x 7 + 2 = _____

2. 60 ÷ 3 − 12 = _____

3. 18 − 2 x 3 = _____

4. 27 + 3 x 2 = _____

5. 2 + 8 ÷ 2 = _____

6. 16 − 6 + 12 = _____

7. 7 − 2 ÷ 1 = _____

8. (24 x 2) − 16 = _____

9. 100 − (200 ÷ 4) = _____

10. -8 + (4 x 5) = _____

11. -9 + (10 ÷ 2) = _____

12. 50 ÷ 5 − 40 = _____

13. $\frac{2}{3} + \left(4 \times \frac{1}{2} \right) =$ _____

14. $-5 \times \left(4 \div \frac{1}{6} \right) =$ _____

15. $-40 \times \left[\frac{3}{4} + \left(2 \div \frac{1}{2} \right) \right] =$ _____

16. [(20 x 15) − (15 x 10) + -50] = _____

17. $2\frac{1}{8} - \left(\frac{5}{6} \times \frac{1}{8} \right) + 1 =$ _____

18. [62 + 78 x 2 − 200 + (80 − 45)] = _____

19. $\left[\left(-\frac{35}{40} \right) + \left(-\frac{25}{20} \right) + \left(-\frac{5}{9} \right) \right] \times 2 =$ _____

20. (222 − 22 + 202 x 2 + 12 x 2) − 202 = _____

21. {201 − [68 − (40 ÷ 4) + (-8) + (70 x 2)]} = _____

22. 1,000 − {[70 − (25 + 22) + (40 ÷ 2) − 12] x 2} = _____

Name: _____ Date: _____

Section **6** Order of Operations

EXTRA PRACTICE Solve the expressions using order of operations rules.

1. 8 x 8 + 6 = _____

2. 30 ÷ 2 – 15 = _____

3. 16 – 3 x 2 = _____

4. 28 + 2 x 4 = _____

5. 3 + 7 ÷ 2 = _____

6. 18 – 8 + 15 = _____

7. 8 – 3 ÷ 1 = _____

8. (25 x 4) – 12 = _____

9. 200 – (500 ÷ 5) = _____

10. -6 + (6 x 3) = _____

11. -8 + (12 ÷ 6) = _____

12. 30 ÷ 3 – 40 = _____

13. $\frac{3}{5} + \left(5 \times \frac{1}{5}\right)$ = _____

14. -6 x $\left(5 \times \frac{1}{6}\right)$ = _____

15. -50 x $\left[\frac{2}{3} + (3 + 5)\right]$ = _____

16. $\frac{17}{8} - \left(\frac{7}{8} \times \frac{1}{2}\right) + 1$ = _____

17. [(30 x 15) – (15 x 20) + -35] = _____

18. [65 + 89 x 3 – 500 + (90 – 45)] = _____

19. (500 – 55 + 505 x 5 + 15 x 5) – 505 = _____

20. {601 – [78 – (50 ÷ 5) + (-5) + (90 x 4)]} = _____

Name: _____

Date: _____

Section Review **1** Covering Sections 1 Through 6

APPLY   For each number, list all factors or identify it as being prime.

1. 36 _____

2. 41 _____

3. 56 _____

4. 60 _____

Add or subtract as indicated. Reduce answers to lowest terms.

5. $\frac{1}{9} + \frac{13}{9} =$ _____

6. $\frac{6}{7} - \frac{3}{4} =$ _____

7. $3 - \frac{12}{15} =$ _____

8. $3\frac{3}{4} + \frac{5}{8} =$ _____

9. $\frac{34}{4} - 1 =$ _____

10. $\frac{1}{22} - \frac{1}{88} =$ _____

11. $5\frac{4}{5} + 3\frac{7}{8} + \frac{1}{2} =$ _____

Multiply or divide as indicated. Reduce answers to lowest terms.

12. $\frac{1}{9} \times \frac{3}{6} =$ _____

13. $\frac{4}{7} \div \frac{1}{4} =$ _____

14. $\frac{3}{8} \times \frac{2}{8} =$ _____

15. $2\frac{7}{12} \times \frac{12}{5} =$ _____

16. $6 \div \frac{1}{4} =$ _____

17. $1\frac{3}{4} \times 7\frac{1}{2} =$ _____

18. $\left(3 \times \frac{1}{2}\right) - \left(2 \times \frac{1}{10}\right) =$ _____

Add or subtract as indicated.

19. $4 + \text{-}5 =$ _____

20. $1 - \text{-}12 =$ _____

21. $\text{-}15 + \text{-}12 =$ _____

22. $\text{-}10 - 0 =$ _____

Multiply or divide as indicated.

23. $2 \times \text{-}2 =$ _____

24. $\text{-}8 \div 1 =$ _____

25. $0 \times \text{-}14 =$ _____

26. $\text{-}45 \times \text{-}10 =$ _____

27. $\text{-}2 \times (18 \times \text{-}8) =$ _____

Name: _____   Date: _____

Section Review **1** Covering Sections 1 Through 6

Solve the expressions using rules for order of operations.

28. 30 x 2 – 1 = _____   **29.** 12 – 3 x 4 = _____

30. 5 + 7 x 2 = _____   **31.** 60 – 3 x 14 = _____

32. 9 ÷ 3 x 8 = _____   **33.** 4 x 8 ÷ 2 + 3 = _____

34. (40 ÷ -10) + (20 x 3) = _____

35. {[1,200 – (120 ÷ 10) + 60] + 200} = _____

36. [34 x (10 – 2)] + [28 x (50 ÷ -5)] = _____

Solve.

37. George wrote a check to a merchant for $87.55, but there was only $22.15 in his bank account. How much money does the account lack in clearing this check?

_____

38. Helen owes $420 on her department store charge account. She plans to make a payment of $45. How much more money would she need to pay off the entire debt?

_____

39. Of the 1,200 people who entered the stadium, only $\frac{1}{8}$ paid the highest ticket price. The rest had discount tickets or bought seats in cheaper sections. How many people paid the highest ticket price?

_____

40. In a recent election, only $\frac{1}{3}$ of the city's 24,600 registered voters showed up on election day to cast their votes. How many people voted in this election?

_____

Name: _____ Date: _____

Section Review **1** Covering Sections 1 Through 6

EXTRA PRACTICE   For each number, list all factors or identify it as being prime.

1. 48 _____ **2.** 50 _____

3. 79 _____ **4.** 98 _____

Add or subtract as indicated. Reduce answers to lowest terms.

5. $\frac{1}{6} + \frac{15}{6} =$ _____ **6.** $\frac{4}{5} - \frac{3}{4} =$ _____

7. $5 - \frac{13}{15} =$ _____ **8.** $\frac{15}{4} + \frac{5}{9} =$ _____

9. $7\frac{2}{3} - 1\frac{1}{6} =$ _____ **10.** $\frac{9}{7} + \frac{1}{5} =$ _____

11. $\frac{2}{15} + \frac{2}{3} =$ _____ **12.** $1\frac{4}{10} - \frac{3}{5} =$ _____

Multiply or divide as indicated. Reduce answers to lowest terms.

13. $\frac{1}{8} \times \frac{5}{6} =$ _____ **14.** $\frac{5}{8} \div \frac{1}{4} =$ _____

15. $\frac{4}{8} \times \frac{3}{8} =$ _____ **16.** $2 \div \frac{2}{3} =$ _____

17. $6\frac{4}{9} \times \frac{3}{5} =$ _____ **18.** $2\frac{1}{3} \div \frac{1}{9} =$ _____

19. $\frac{7}{16} \div \frac{4}{6} =$ _____ **20.** $8 \times \frac{5}{12} =$ _____

Add, subtract, multiply, or divide as indicated. Use the proper order of operations. Reduce answers to lowest terms if needed.

21. $3 + -6 =$ _____ **22.** $13 - -12 =$ _____

23. $2 \times -3 =$ _____ **24.** $-7 \div 1 =$ _____

25. $50 \times 3 - 2 =$ _____ **26.** $18 - 6 \times 4 =$ _____

27. $5 + 4 \times 3 =$ _____ **28.** $70 - 5 \times 15 =$ _____

29. $-\frac{4}{5} \times \frac{6}{10} =$ _____ **30.** $10 \div -\frac{3}{8} =$ _____

Name: _____   Date: _____

Section Review Covering Sections 1 Through 6

31. $6 \times \left(\frac{5}{8} - \frac{2}{8}\right) =$ _____

32. $\frac{1}{4} + \frac{1}{5} \div \frac{1}{6} =$ _____

33. $\left(-\frac{7}{10} + \frac{3}{5}\right) - 4 =$ _____

34. $\frac{6}{7} \times -\frac{1}{2} \times -\frac{2}{3} =$ _____

35. $\{870 - [(60 \times 8) + 14]\} \div 2 =$ _____

36. $[(19 + 3) \times 3] + [22 \div (7 + 4)] =$ _____

Solve.

37. Bob used his debit card to make a purchase for $125.75, but there was only $72.50 in his bank account. What will be the balance of his account after the purchase?

_____

38. Jenna owes $550 on her credit card. She is planning on making a payment of $25. What will be the balance of her account after the payment?

_____

39. Big Time Music ordered 960 CDs to stock up for the holidays. In the shipment, $\frac{1}{12}$ of the CDs were damaged when the delivery truck was involved in an accident. How many CDs were damaged?

_____

40. If $\frac{2}{3}$ of a class of 27 students passed the last math test, how many students failed?

_____

Section 7 Squares and Square Roots

ABSORB

Squaring or **taking a number's square** are terms that mean multiplying a number by itself. If we take the number 7 and square it, it is the same as saying 7 x 7. The common way of writing "7 squared" is 7^2. The small raised number (called an **exponent**) signifies that 7 is to be multiplied by itself that number of times. Consider the following examples of squaring a number:

Example 1: $4^2 =$

$4 \times 4 =$

$4 \times 4 = 16$

Example 2: $10^2 =$

$10 \times 10 =$

$10 \times 10 = 100$

Taking a **square root** of a number is essentially the reverse process of squaring that number. For instance, consider the number 49. We know that 7 x 7 = 49, so the square root of 49 is 7. Often though, the square root of a number is not a nice, neat whole number. The $\sqrt{}$ is called a **radical sign** and indicates that you should find the square root of a number.

Example 3: $\sqrt{64} =$

Since 8 x 8 = 64, the square root of 64 is 8.

A calculator is recommended for working with square roots when the numbers are not perfect squares such as 64 or 16.

Example 4: $\sqrt{30} =$

$\sqrt{30} = 5.4772256$

As you can see, the square root of 30 turns out to be a somewhat strange-looking number that runs many places past the decimal. It makes sense that the square root of 30 will be a number between 5 and 6 since 5 x 5 = 25 and 6 x 6 = 36. For the purpose of our work here, writing four places past the decimal point and rounding off will be sufficient.

Name: _____ Date: _____

Section **7** Squares and Square Roots

APPLY Find the square of each number.

1. 5^2 _____

2. 4^2 _____

3. 11^2 _____

4. 2^2 _____

5. 16^2 _____

6. 20^2 _____

7. 1^2 _____

8. 3.4^2 _____

9. 8.8^2 _____

10. $\frac{1}{4}^2$ _____

11. $2\frac{1}{2}^2$ _____

12. $\frac{7}{8}^2$ _____

Find the square root of each number. It is only necessary to work to four places past the decimal point in expressing answers. Round off the answers, if necessary. A calculator is recommended for this activity.

13. $\sqrt{64}$ _____

14. $\sqrt{36}$ _____

15. $\sqrt{81}$ _____

16. $\sqrt{70}$ _____

17. $\sqrt{125}$ _____

18. $\sqrt{220}$ _____

19. $\sqrt{900}$ _____

20. $\sqrt{1,200}$ _____

Name: _____ Date: _____

Section **7** Squares and Square Roots

EXTRA PRACTICE   Find the square of each number.

1. 8^2 _____

2. 6^2 _____

3. 12^2 _____

4. 3^2 _____

5. 15^2 _____

6. 30^2 _____

7. 4.5^2 _____

8. 6.6^2 _____

9. $\frac{1}{3}^2$ _____

10. $3\frac{1}{4}^2$ _____

Find the square root of each number. It is only necessary to work to four places past the decimal point in expressing answers. Round off the answers, if necessary. A calculator is recommended for this activity.

11. $\sqrt{62}$ _____

12. $\sqrt{24}$ _____

13. $\sqrt{49}$ _____

14. $\sqrt{88}$ _____

15. $\sqrt{122}$ _____

16. $\sqrt{36}$ _____

17. $\sqrt{100}$ _____

18. $\sqrt{428}$ _____

19. $\sqrt{1,225}$ _____

20. $\sqrt{3,817}$ _____

Section **8** Exponents

ABSORB In the previous section, we learned that a number may be squared simply by multiplying it by itself. $7 \times 7 = 7^2$ is an example of squaring, and the ^{2} in this example is an **exponent**. The raised number exponent simply tells how many times a base number is to be multiplied by itself. In this example, the 7 was the **base number**.

Base numbers and exponents essentially work the same way as squaring, except the exponent determines how many times the base number is to be multiplied by itself. Consider the number 20^5. This could be rewritten as $20 \times 20 \times 20 \times 20 \times 20$. Once multiplied out, this would be 3,200,000. You can see from this example that a relatively small exponent increases a base number greatly through the power of multiplication. This fast rate of increase is commonly referred to as **exponential growth**.

Example 1: 4^3

$4 \times 4 \times 4 =$

$4 \times 4 \times 4 = 64$

Example 2: 2^4

$2 \times 2 \times 2 \times 2 =$

$2 \times 2 \times 2 \times 2 = 16$

Example 3: 10^4

$10 \times 10 \times 10 \times 10 =$

$10 \times 10 \times 10 \times 10 = 10,000$

A calculator can provide a fast answer for what could be an otherwise time-consuming process, especially if there is a large base number/exponent combination involved. Most math/scientific calculators have a y^x key that makes solving for the value much faster. On most calculators:

1. enter the base number,
2. press the y^x key,
3. then enter the exponent
4. and press the = key.

Name: _____ Date: _____

Section **8** Exponents

APPLY   Write the number equivalent for each base number and exponent. Your teacher may allow you to use a calculator for this activity.

1. $2^6 =$ _____

2. $4^4 =$ _____

3. $9^3 =$ _____

4. $12^3 =$ _____

5. $50^2 =$ _____

6. $7^5 =$ _____

7. $16^2 =$ _____

8. $15^3 =$ _____

Rewrite each expression as a base number with exponent.

9. 25 x 25 x 25 x 25 x 25 = _____

10. 10 x 10 x 10 x 10 x 10 = _____

11. 4 x 4 x 4 x 4 x 4 x 4 x 4 = _____

12. 120 x 120 x 120 = _____

For each number given, try to determine how it might be rewritten as a base number with exponent.

13. 27 = _____

14. 32 = _____

15. 125 = _____

16. 1,000 = _____

Name: _____ Date: _____

Section **8** Exponents

EXTRA PRACTICE   Write the number equivalent for each base number and exponent. Your teacher may allow you to use a calculator for this activity.

1. $3^5 =$ _____

2. $3^3 =$ _____

3. $9^4 =$ _____

4. $15^4 =$ _____

5. $25^2 =$ _____

6. $8^3 =$ _____

7. $14^5 =$ _____

8. $18^2 =$ _____

Rewrite each expression as a base number with exponent.

9. 50 x 50 x 50 x 50 = _____

10. 12 x 12 x 12 = _____

11. 2 x 2 x 2 x 2 x 2 x 2 x 2 = _____

12. 100 x 100 x 100 x 100 x 100 = _____

For each number given, try to determine how it might be rewritten as a base number with exponent.

13. 25 = _____

14. 36 = _____

15. 1,728 = _____

16. 10,000 = _____

Name: _____   Date: _____

Section 9 | What Is a Variable?

ABSORB   Consider the following equation. $24 - 18 =$

This equation can be solved quite easily by performing the subtraction indicated. The answer, of course, is 6. But what if this equation represented quantities that were not known? What if the 18 stood for the price of a store item that was not known until it was shopped for? What if the 24 was a quantity of money that was not known until the contents of a piggy bank were counted out in full?

In mathematics, there are ways of working with numbers that are not known. A variable provides a method for working with quantities that are not known. A **variable** is usually a lowercase, italicized letter that appears in math expressions or equations, just as if it were a number. Consider the following examples.

Example 1:   some quantity of boxes to be shipped

   y boxes or simply expressed as y

Example 2:   all the animals in an entire zoo

   x animals or simply expressed as x

APPLY   Select a variable to name the quantities described.

1. the number of students that attend a school _____

2. the amount of water in a large tank _____

3. the number of crates stacked in a warehouse _____

4. the amount of gasoline needed to fly a plane between two cities _____

5. the number of people who applied for a job opening _____

6. the number of passengers that can be carried by a bus _____

7. the gallons of milk a dairy produces on a daily basis _____

8. the number of bales of hay a truck can carry _____

Section 10 Expressions With Variables

ABSORB Consider the following examples of evaluating basic expressions involving variables.

Example 1: $24 - y$, with $y = 3$

becomes $24 - 3$

solved 21

Example 2: $t + 20$, with $t = 15$

becomes $15 + 20$

solved 35

Example 3: $100 - d$, with $d = 29$

becomes $100 - 29$

solved 71

Working with variables can be fairly easy when simple expressions are involved and values have been provided for the variable, as with the examples above. But working with variables as part of an equation often requires us to solve for the value of the variable, since the variable's value may not be provided.

Consider the examples below involving variables in equations.

Example 4: $r + 10 = 18$

Think about what number, when added to 10, would yield 18.

$8 + 10 = 18$

so in this equation, $r = 8$

Example 5: $y - 15 = 4$

Think about what number, when 15 is subtracted, would yield 4.

$19 - 15 = 4$

so in this equation, $y = 19$

Name: _____   Date: _____

Section **10** Expressions With Variables

APPLY   Evaluate the expressions with the values provided.

1. $a + 5$, $a = 17$ _____

2. $t - 17$, $t = 23$ _____

3. $f + 24$, $f = 9$ _____

4. $40 + h$, $h = 24$ _____

5. $b - 24$, $b = 10$ _____

6. $20 - w$, $w = 20$ _____

7. $g - 2$, $g = 3$ _____

8. $k - 5\frac{1}{2}$, $k = 7\frac{1}{4}$ _____

9. $w + 2 + y$, $w = 4$ and $y = 16$ _____

10. $(c - 12) + y$, $c = 22$ and $y = 9$ _____

Solve for the value of the variables in each equation.

11. $3 + w = 12$, $w = $ _____

12. $t - 12 = 0$, $t = $ _____

13. $45 - j = 13$, $j = $ _____

14. $p - 7 = 14$, $p = $ _____

15. $k - 23 = 13$, $k = $ _____

16. $y + 14 = 0$, $y = $ _____

17. $q + 1 = 0$, $q = $ _____

18. $m + 8 = 0$, $m = $ _____

19. $c + 24 + 14 = 38$, $c = $ _____

20. $4 - y + 1 = 3\frac{1}{2}$, $y = $ _____

21. $w - \left(2\frac{1}{3} - 1\frac{2}{3}\right) = 0$, $w = $ _____

22. $27 - r = 34 - 12$, $r = $ _____

Name: _____ Date: _____

Section ⑩ Expressions With Variables

EXTRA PRACTICE   Evaluate the expressions with the values provided.

1. $x + 6$, $x = 7$ _____ **2.** $z - 20$, $z = 25$ _____

3. $a + 25$, $a = 10$ _____ **4.** $50 + b$, $b = 30$ _____

5. $c - 55$, $c = 15$ _____ **6.** $25 - d$, $d = 35$ _____

7. $f - 1$, $f = 2$ _____ **8.** $g - 11\frac{1}{2}$, $g = 10\frac{3}{4}$ _____

9. $h + 5 + i$, $h = 3$ and $i = 15$ _____

10. $(j - 10) + k$, $j = 25$ and $k = 12$ _____

Solve for the value of the variables in each equation.

11. $5 + w = 15$, $w = $ _____ **12.** $t - 10 = 3$, $t = $ _____

13. $50 - j = 20$, $j = $ _____ **14.** $p - 8 = 15$, $p = $ _____

15. $k - 25 = 12$, $k = $ _____ **16.** $y + 13 = 0$, $y = $ _____

17. $q + 2 = 3$, $q = $ _____ **18.** $m + 9 = 5$, $m = $ _____

19. $c + 25 + 15 = 40$, $c = $ _____ **20.** $5 - y + 3 = 4\frac{1}{4}$, $y = $ _____

21. $w - \left(6\frac{5}{6} - 2\frac{1}{6}\right) = 2$, $w = $ _____ **22.** $19 - r = 28 - 14$, $r = $ _____

Section 11 More Practice With Variables

ABSORB

In the previous section, it was shown that simple equations involving variables may be solved by inspection or even by substituting reasonable numbers until the correct one is found. Many equations and expressions involving variables aren't in a simplified form, however. Combining **like terms** is a way of simplifying expressions or equations in order to make solving them easier.

Before looking at the examples, we need to review an important rule for variables that will making working with them easier.

For the variable y: $\quad y = 1y$

$$y + y = 2y$$

$$y + y + y = 3y$$

$$y + y + y + y = 4y$$

This pattern continues on and on for any quantity of y. This rule works because the variable y behaves the same as any number. For instance, $4 + 4 + 4 = 12$, and we know also that $3 \times 4 = 12$. It follows then that if y is added a certain number of times, then it is the same as multiplying. Multiplying is really adding over and over again, isn't it? In this section, we'll concentrate on simplifying expressions rather than solving equations.

Also, when working with variables, it is understood that a number placed next to a variable with no sign placed between the two always means **multiplication**.

Example 1: $\quad r + 2r + 5 + 50$

Combine like variables and numbers;

$3r + 55 \qquad$ is the simplified form.

Example 2: $\quad 40 + 4g - 3g - 25$

Combine like variables and numbers;

$g + 15 \qquad$ is the simplified form.

Example 3: $\quad t - 23 + 14 - 3t$

Combine like variables and numbers;

$-2t - 9 \qquad$ is the simplified form.

Name: _____   Date: _____

Section **11** More Practice With Variables

APPLY   Simplify each expression by combining like terms.

1. $k - 12 + k + k + 15$ _____

2. $14y + 4 - 11y - 18$ _____

3. $4h - 2h + 17 - 2h + 4 - 14$ _____

4. $20c - 12c + 48 + 2c - 64 - 6c$ _____

5. $3k + 45 - k + 25 - 2k$ _____

6. $24 - k - 24 + k$ _____

7. $23n - 20n + 100 - 22n - 120$ _____

8. $16f - 12f + 2f + 6f - 60f + 120f$ _____

9. $240 - 24t - 4t + 120 - 16t + 36t - 140$ _____

10. $80 + 40r - 20r + 16r - 48 + 60r - 64$ _____

Simplify each expression, and then evaluate the expression for the value given.

11. $y + y + 1 + 3 + y - 16 - 2y,\ y = 3$ _____

12. $t - 2t + 2\frac{1}{4} + 3t,\ t = \frac{1}{2}$ _____

13. $120 - 4y + 30 - 12,\ y = 2$ _____

14. $6w - 2w - 88 + 16w - 18,\ w = 3$ _____

15. $k + 3k - 44 + 24 + k,\ k = 2$ _____

Name: _____ Date: _____

Section **11** More Practice With Variables

EXTRA PRACTICE   Simplify each expression by combining like terms.

1. $x - 15 + x + x + 20$ _____

2. $20y + 5 - 15y - 19$ _____

3. $5z - 3z + 13 - z + 5 - 15$ _____

4. $25d - 15d + 50 + 3d - 65 - 7d$ _____

5. $2k + 50 - 2k + 25 - 3k$ _____

6. $30 - m - 26 + m$ _____

7. $24n - 19n + 200 - 23n - 150$ _____

8. $15f - 13f + 3f + 7f - 50f + 150f$ _____

9. $250 - 25r - 5r + 150 - 17r + 37r - 120$ _____

10. $90 + 50g - 30g + 17g - 50 + 60g - 65$ _____

11. $7a - 3a + 5 + 2a - 6$ _____

12. $32 + 15 + 9s + 41s - 6s - 17$ _____

13. $-6 + 8n - 2n + 20 + 11n$ _____

14. $19q - 7q + 6q - 14 + 89$ _____

15. $5d + 9d + 12d - 15d + 27 - 5$ _____

Name: _____ Date: _____

Section **11** More Practice With Variables

EXTRA PRACTICE Simplify each expression, and then evaluate the expression for the value given.

1. $q + q + 2 + 4 + q - 17$, $q = 5$ _____

2. $f - 3f + 2\frac{1}{2} + 5f$, $f = 1\frac{1}{2}$ _____

3. $150 - 5d + 25 - 15$, $d = 3$ _____

4. $7w - 6w - 99 + 15w - 20$, $w = 10$ _____

5. $v + 5v - 55 + 25 + v$, $v = 7$ _____

6. $2w + w + 5 + 8 + 3w - 17 - 8w$, $w = 15$ _____

7. $z - 9z + 5\frac{3}{4} + 5z$, $z = 8$ _____

8. $220 - 9t + 35 - 14$, $t = 7$ _____

9. $9h - 3h - 77 + 20h - 16$, $h = 10$ _____

10. $m + 6m - 88 + 50 + m$, $m = 24$ _____

Name: _____

Date: _____

Section Review (2) Covering Sections 1 Through 11

APPLY   List all factors for each number. Write "prime" if the number has only 1 and itself as factors.

1. 6   _____

2. 21   _____

3. 40   _____

4. 51   _____

5. 74   _____

6. 128   _____

7. 250   _____

Add or subtract as indicated. Reduce answers to lowest terms.

8. $\frac{2}{4} + \frac{3}{4} =$ _____

9. $\frac{4}{5} - \frac{1}{20} =$ _____

10. $1\frac{2}{3} - \frac{2}{9} =$ _____

11. $\frac{7}{8} + \frac{7}{9} =$ _____

12. $4\frac{1}{4} - \frac{5}{9} =$ _____

13. $8 - 3\frac{3}{5} =$ _____

14. $\frac{40}{50} + \frac{40}{50} + 1\frac{20}{50} =$ _____

15. $\left(\frac{13}{8} - \frac{1}{3}\right) + \frac{7}{24} =$ _____

Multiply or divide as indicated. Reduce answers to lowest terms.

16. $\frac{3}{4} \times \frac{3}{4} =$ _____

17. $\frac{3}{10} \div \frac{3}{4} =$ _____

18. $4 \div \frac{1}{8} =$ _____

19. $3\frac{3}{4} \times \frac{7}{8} =$ _____

20. $5\frac{6}{16} \times 2 =$ _____

21. $100 \times \frac{2}{3} =$ _____

22. $\left(1\frac{4}{5} \times \frac{2}{3}\right) \times 3 =$ _____

Name: _____   Date: _____

Section Review **2** Covering Sections 1 Through 11

Add or subtract as indicated. Reduce answers to lowest terms.

23. 2 + -2 = _____   **24.** -8 + 2 = _____

25. 0 – 12 = _____   **26.** -12 + 2 = _____

27. -15 + 15 = _____   **28.** -5 + -7 = _____

29. 8 – -6 = _____   **30.** -11 – -18 = _____

31. $\frac{1}{2} - -\frac{1}{4}$ = _____   **32.** $-\frac{3}{4} + -4$ = _____

Multiply or divide as indicated. Reduce answers to lowest terms.

33. 10 x -6 = _____   **34.** -6 x 6 = _____

35. -30 x -3 = _____   **36.** 24 ÷ -24 = _____

37. $\frac{3}{4}$ x $-\frac{3}{4}$ = _____   **38.** $1\frac{1}{4}$ x -8 = _____

39. -4 ÷ $\frac{1}{12}$ = _____   **40.** $-\frac{4}{7} ÷ -\frac{1}{2}$ = _____

Solve the expressions using order of operations rules.

41. 3 x 3 + 7 = _____   **42.** 4 + 3 x 12 = _____

43. 100 ÷ 2 + 50 = _____   **44.** 100 – 8 ÷ 4 = _____

45. (100 – 55) x (100 ÷ 25) = _____

46. $\left[75 - \left(20 \text{ x } \frac{1}{2}\right) + (60 ÷ 4) + -22\right]$ = _____

Find the square root of each number. It is only necessary to work to four places past the decimal point and round off in expressing answers. Use a calculator if needed.

47. 24 _____   **48.** 64 _____

49. 84 _____   **50.** 71 _____

Name: _____   Date: _____

Section Review 2 Covering Sections 1 Through 11

Write the number equivalent.

51. $4^2 = $ _____

52. $6^3 = $ _____

Rewrite each expression as a base number with exponent.

53. 30 x 30 x 30 x 30 x 30 = _____

54. 12 x 12 x 12 x 12 = _____

55. 6 x 6 x 6 x 6 x 6 x 6 x 6 = _____

Evaluate the expressions with the values provided.

56. $t - 4$, $t = 12$ _____

57. $y + 4$, $y = -2$ _____

58. $q + 1$, $q = 0$ _____

59. $k + 12$, $k = -6$ _____

Solve for the value of the variable.

60. $4 - y = 4$, $y = $ _____

61. $22 - w = 9$, $w = $ _____

62. $t + 4 = 0$, $t = $ _____

63. $54 - y = 14$, $y = $ _____

Simplify each expression by combining like terms.

64. $r + 2r + 12 + r - 8 = $ _____

65. $3h - 2h + 12 - h + 14 - 7 + 4h = $ _____

66. $40 - 20y + 80 + 60y - 30 - 20y - 40 = $ _____

Name: _____ Date: _____

Section Review ② Covering Sections 1 Through 11

EXTRA PRACTICE   List all factors for each number. Write "prime" if the number has only 1 and itself as factors.

1. 7 _____

2. 22 _____

3. 35 _____

4. 50 _____

Add or subtract as indicated. Reduce answers to the lowest terms.

5. $\frac{2}{5} + \frac{3}{5} =$ _____

6. $\frac{6}{10} - \frac{1}{30} =$ _____

7. $\frac{5}{3} - \frac{7}{9} =$ _____

8. $\frac{5}{8} + \frac{6}{9} =$ _____

Multiply or divide as indicated. Reduce answers to lowest terms.

9. $\frac{5}{9} \times \frac{5}{9} =$ _____

10. $\frac{6}{10} \div \frac{2}{3} =$ _____

11. $5 \div \frac{1}{9} =$ _____

12. $\frac{15}{4} \times \frac{3}{8} =$ _____

Add or subtract as indicated.

13. 3 + -3 = _____

14. -9 + 3 = _____

15. 0 – 15 = _____

16. -12 + 3 = _____

17. -12 + 12 = _____

Multiply or divide as indicated.

18. 10 x -5 = _____

19. -8 x 8 = _____

20. -20 x -2 = _____

21. 25 ÷ -25 = _____

Solve the expressions using order of operations rules.

22. 2 x 2 + 8 = _____

23. 5 + 3 x 15 = _____

24. 200 ÷ 5 x 25 = _____

Name: _____ Date: _____

Section Review **2** Covering Sections 1 Through 11

Find the square root of each number. It is only necessary to work to four places past the decimal point and round off in expressing answers. Use a calculator if needed.

25. 25 _____

26. 60 _____

27. 105 _____

28. 81 _____

Find the number equivalent.

29. 5^2 = _____

30. 2^6 = _____

31. 7^4 = _____

32. 4^7 = _____

Rewrite each expression as a base number with exponent.

33. 20 x 20 x 20 x 20 x 20 = _____

34. 15 x 15 x 15 = _____

35. 2 x 2 x 2 x 2 x 2 x 2 x 2 x 2 = _____

36. 40 x 40 = _____

Evaluate the expressions with the values provided.

37. $x - 5$, $x = 15$ _____

38. $y + 3$, $y = -3$ _____

39. $17 - b$, $b = -5$ _____

40. $n + 33$, $n = 13$ _____

Solve for the value of the variable.

41. $5 - z = 2$, $z = $ _____

42. $55 - g = 8$, $g = $ _____

43. $m + 19 = 8$, $m = $ _____

44. $24 + t = 35$, $t = $ _____

Simplify each expression by combining like terms.

45. $a + 3a + 15 + a - 9 = $ _____

46. $5f - 4f + 15 - f + 20 - 8 + 6f = $ _____

47. $16 + 3s + s - 12 + 7s - 4s + 6 = $ _____

48. $-9y + 14 + 7y - 8 + 20y - 5 + 16 - 2y = $ _____

Section 12 Perimeter and Area

ABSORB Perimeter and area represent very different types of measures. Perimeter is a measure of length. The **perimeter** of a figure is a measure of the length for the exterior of that figure. Consider the figure shown at the right.

Put your pencil point at one of the corners of this figure and trace your pencil all the way around the figure, following the sides exactly, back to your starting point. You have just traced the perimeter of this figure. For **polygons** (multi-sided figures with straight lines for sides), the perimeter is found by adding the lengths of all the sides.

Example 1:

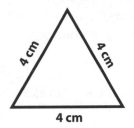

side + side + side = perimeter

4 cm + 4 cm + 4 cm = perimeter

4 cm + 4 cm + 4 cm = 12 cm

The perimeter of this triangle is 12 cm.

Recall that for any polygon, such as squares, rectangles, triangles, pentagons, etc., the perimeter is found by simply adding the lengths of all sides.

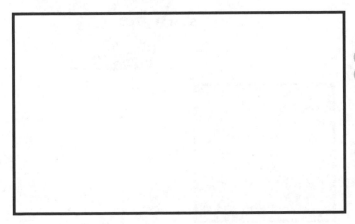

Area is a different kind of measurement than perimeter. **Area** is a measure of a flat space, such as a tabletop or the amount of floor space in a room. Consider the figure at the left.

Put your pencil point in the interior of the region and shade in the enclosed area. This interior portion of the figure is its area. For **squares and rectangles**, the area is found by multiplying the length times the width.

Name: _____ Date: _____

Section **12** Perimeter and Area

Example 2:

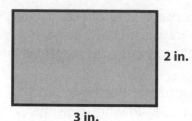

2 in.

3 in.

length x width = area

3 in. x 2 in. = area

3 in. x 2 in. = 6 square inches or 6 in.^{2}
        (Area is always expressed in terms of square units,
        such as square inches, square centimeters, etc.)

APPLY   Determine the perimeter for each of the figures shown below.

1. perimeter = _____

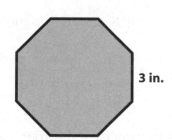

3 in.

2. perimeter = _____

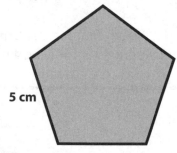

5 cm

3. perimeter = _____

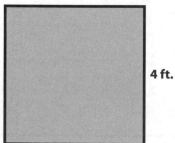

4 ft.

Name: _____ Date: _____

Section **12** Perimeter and Area

Determine the area for each of the figures below.

4. area = _____

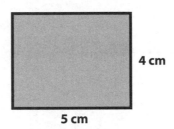

4 cm

5 cm

5. area = _____

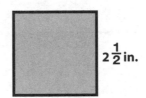

$2\frac{1}{2}$ in.

6. area = _____

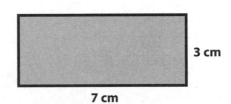

3 cm

7 cm

CONSIDER THIS

    In previous sections, it was shown how variables may be used in place of numbers in math expressions. The formula for the perimeter of this rectangle could be written in this way:

       L + *L* + *W* + *W* = **Perimeter**

    simplified 2*L* + 2*W* = *P*

    Likewise, the formula for area can be written this way:

       L x *W* = **Area**

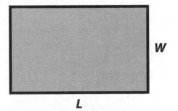

W

L

    These formulas will solve for perimeter and area, regardless of the actual numbers involved.

Name: _____ Date: _____

Section **12** Perimeter and Area

EXTRA PRACTICE Determine the perimeter for each of the figures shown below.

1. perimeter = _____

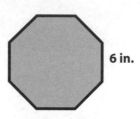
6 in.

2. perimeter = _____

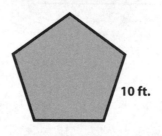
10 cm

3. perimeter = _____

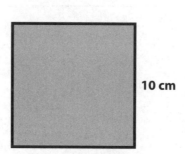
10 ft.

4. perimeter = _____

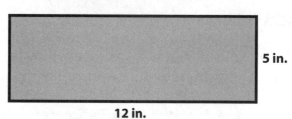
5 in.

12 in.

5. perimeter = _____

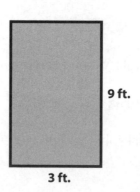
9 ft.

3 ft.

48

Name: _____ Date: _____

Section **12** Perimeter and Area

EXTRA PRACTICE   Determine the area for each of the figures shown below.

1.   area = _____

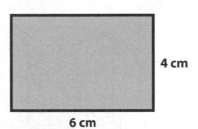
4 cm
6 cm

2.   area = _____

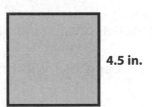
4.5 in.

3.   area = _____

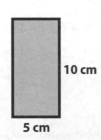
10 cm
5 cm

4.   area = _____

7 ft.

5.   area = _____

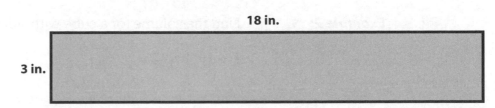
18 in.
3 in.

Section 13 Volume

ABSORB   **Volume** is a measurement of capacity, such as the amount of space there is inside a cardboard box. As with perimeter and area, volume may be found by using a math expression with variables. Consider the drawing below of a rectangular prism.

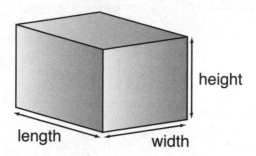

The volume of rectangular prisms (and cubes) may be found by using the following formula:

Length x Width x Height = Volume

$$L \times W \times H = V$$

Volume is always expressed as some amount of cubic units, such as cubic feet, cubic centimeters, etc.

Example 1:

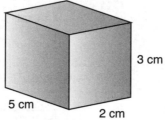

$$L \times W \times H = V$$

$$5\,cm \times 2\,cm \times 3\,cm = V$$

The volume is 30 cubic cm or 30 cm^3.

Example 2:   Find the volume for a cube with sides of 4 inches.

$$L \times W \times H = V$$

$$4\,in. \times 4\,in. \times 4\,in. = V$$

The volume is 64 cubic inches or 64 in.^{3}.

Name: _____   Date: _____

Section **13** Volume

APPLY   Determine the volume for each figure.

1. V = _____

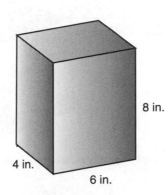

8 in.

4 in.

6 in.

2. V = _____

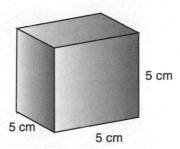

5 cm

5 cm

5 cm

Determine the volume for each of the circumstances described.

3. A warehouse with interior storage dimensions 200 feet in length, 100 feet in width, and a height of 16 feet

    V = _____

4. A railroad boxcar with cargo space of 60 ft. by 12 ft. by 12 ft.

    V = _____

5. A cardboard box with interior dimensions of 24 inches by 24 inches by 36 inches

    V = _____

6. An artist's storage box with interior dimensions of 26 cm, 44 cm, 12 cm

    V = _____

Name: _____ Date: _____

Section **13** Volume

Determine the volume for each figure.

1. *V* = _____

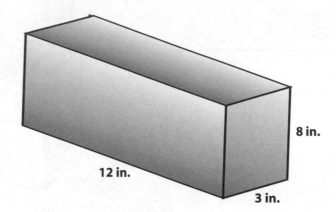

8 in.

12 in.

3 in.

2. *V* = _____

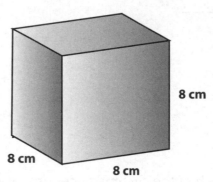

8 cm

8 cm

8 cm

Determine the volume for each of the circumstances described.

3. A garage is 10 feet wide by 25 feet long by 15 feet high

   V = _____

4. A shipping container is 45 feet long, 15 feet wide, and 15 feet high

   V = _____

5. A box is 12 in. by 12 in. by 24 in.

   V = _____

6. A storage tub is 25 cm by 45 cm by 10 cm

   V = _____

15'

10'

25'

Section 14 Working With Circles

ABSORB

As with other figures, the perimeter and area of a circle may be determined using basic formulas. The perimeter of a circle is actually referred to as the **circumference**, but the concept is identical to that of perimeter. Circumference is the distance around the outer edge of the circle.

Consider the illustration below, which shows the radius of a circle.

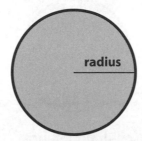

radius

You can see from the illustration that the **radius** is the distance from one edge of the circle to the center. (By definition, the **diameter** is 2 times the length of the radius. A diameter is the distance from one edge of the circle through the center of the circle to the other edge.)

In this section, we'll work with the radius in finding both the circumference and area, but it is quite easy to determine the radius by taking half the diameter if that is the measurement you are given for a problem.

About Pi:

There is one more thing you should know about circles before we begin with the formulas for circumference and area. **Pi** is the name given to a special ratio used for working with circles. The symbol π is used for representing this special number, which is approximated by the number **3.1415** in computations where π is used.

The basic formulas for a circle are:

Circumference: 2 x π x radius = circumference

$2\pi r = C$ (In this simplified formula, you'll notice the multiplication symbols have been left out. It's an understood notation for variables, which we'll begin using at this point.)

$6.283r = C$ (further simplified by multiplying 2π to get a constant number for the formula)

Name: _____   Date: _____

Section **14** Working With Circles

Area: π x (radius x radius) = area

$\pi r^2 = A$ (simplified)

A calculator is recommended for working through the examples and practice section.

Example:

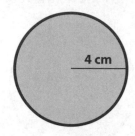

4 cm

Circumference: $2\pi r$ = Circumference

2 (3.1415) 4 cm = C

6.283 (4 cm) = C

25.123 centimeters is the circumference.

Area: πr^2 = Area

(3.1415) 4^2 = A

(3.1415) 16 = A

50.264 square centimeters is the area.

APPLY   Solve for the circumference and area of each circle. Answers should only be expressed to four places past the decimal point and rounded off, where applicable.

1. C = _____

A = _____

7 in.

2. C = _____

A = _____

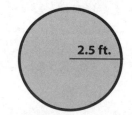

2.5 ft.

Name: _____   Date: _____

Section **14** Working With Circles

3. C = _____

A = _____

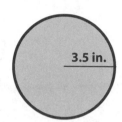

44 cm

4. C = _____

A = _____

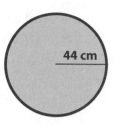

3.5 in.

EXTENDING THE LEARNING

The following problems give the diameter of the circle, so you'll need to convert that figure to the radius before using the formulas for circumference and area.

5. C = _____

A = _____

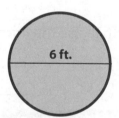

6 ft.

6. C = _____

A = _____

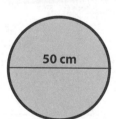

50 cm

7. C = _____

A = _____

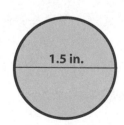

1.5 in.

Name: _____ Date: _____

Section **14** Working With Circles

EXTRA PRACTICE Solve for the circumference and area of each circle. Answers should only be expressed to four places past the decimal point and rounded off, where applicable.

1. C = _____

A = _____

2. C = _____

A = _____

3. C = _____

A = _____

4. C = _____

A = _____

Find the radius using the diameter given, and then use the formulas to find the circumference and area for each circle below.

5. C = _____

A = _____

6. C = _____

A = _____

7. C = _____

A = _____

8. C = _____

A = _____

Name: _____ Date: _____

Section **15** Basic Properties of Numbers

ABSORB Several basic mathematical properties define the way in which numbers behave. Understanding how these properties apply makes it easier to work with and simplify expressions or equations, especially those involving variables. Consider the following properties.

Commutative Property: $6 + 5 = 5 + 6$

   What does this mean in a practical way? It makes it easier to simplify expressions, since terms may be rearranged as long as relationships are not altered.

Associative Property: $(2 \times 4) \times 5 = (5 \times 4) \times 2$

   This allows numbers to be grouped differently with the same result.

Distributive Property: $(3 + 7) \times 5 = (5 \times 3) + (5 \times 7)$

   This provides a way to factor out common terms.

APPLY The problems below contain an expression in each column. Using the properties above, determine whether the expressions are equivalent forms or not. Write "yes" or "no" to denote your answer.

1. $(4 \times 4) \times 5$ $(4 + 4) \times 5$ _____

2. $6 \times (4 + 1)$ $(4 + 1) \times 6$ _____

3. $(8 + 1) \times 2$ $(2 \times 8) + (2 \times 1)$ _____

4. $y + 4$ $4 + y$ _____

5. $2 \times 3 \times 5$ $2 \times (3 + 5)$ _____

6. $(6 \times 7) + (6 \times 2)$ $6 \times (7 + 2)$ _____

7. $1 \times (4 + 5)$ $1 \times (5 + 4)$ _____

8. $n + a + b$ $b \times a \times n$ _____

9. $a + b + c$ $c + b + a$ _____

10. $9 \times (m + n)$ $9m + 9n$ _____

Name: _____ Date: _____

Section 15 Basic Properties of Numbers

EXTRA PRACTICE The problems below contain an expression in each column. Using the properties on the previous page, determine whether the expressions are equivalent forms or not. Write "yes" or "no" to denote your answer.

1.	(5 x 5) x 6	(5 + 5) x 6	_____
2.	7 x (5 + 1)	(5 + 1) x 6	_____
3.	(9 + 2) x 3	(1 x 9) + (3 x 1)	_____
4.	z + 5	5 + z	_____
5.	3 x 4 x 6	3 x (4 + 6)	_____
6.	(6 x 8) + (6 x 3)	6 x (8 + 3)	_____
7.	2 x (5 + 6)	2 x (6 + 5)	_____
8.	q + p + c	(p + c) x q	_____
9.	(s + t) x 5	5s + 5t	_____
10.	e x f x g	f x g x e	_____

Identify which property is demonstrated by each pair of expressions below: commutative property, associative property, or distributive property.

11.	(7 x 3) x 2	(2 x 3) x 7	_____
12.	a + b	b + a	_____
13.	(8 + 2) + 6	(2 + 6) + 8	_____
14.	10 x (d + g)	10d + 10g	_____
15.	9 x 7	7 x 9	_____

Section 16 Studying Data

ABSORB   **Data** is basically information in the form of numbers. Data can be a group of test scores, population information, or even the way votes were cast in an election.

The mean, median, and mode are three common measures of data. These measures allow a body of data to be seen from different perspectives. Mean, median, and mode give different information about a set of data without having to reexamine the entire data group. This can be important, for instance, if you have a group of 2,000 scores given on a particular college entrance exam. Maybe you only want to know some general information about how people did on the exam without having to sift through and study 2,000 test papers. That's where measures like mean, median, and mode become useful.

Median is the middle item in a data set, easily found by arranging the numbers in the set from least to greatest. Then determine the center number in the data set (or find the average of the two center numbers if there is an even number of data set members).

Mode is the data set member that repeats most often. (Sometimes there is no mode.)

Mean is commonly called the average. It is found by adding all members of the data set and then dividing that sum by how many members are in the data set.

Example: The weights in pounds of patients visiting a diet clinic: 148, 202, 148, 206, 300.

Step one: Rewrite in order from least to greatest:

148, 148, 202, 206, 300

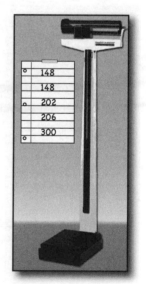

202 is the median, since it is in the center of this data set if you count from either end back to the center.

Step two: Look for identical data set members:

148, 148, 202, 206, 300

148 is the mode, since it is the only data set member that is repeated.

Step three: Add the data set members and divide their sum by the number of set members:

148 + 148 + 202 + 206 + 300 = 1,004

1,004 ÷ 5 = 200.8 lbs. This is the mean.

Name: _____ Date: _____

Section 16 Studying Data

APPLY Find the median, mode, and mean for each data set. Round answers off to four places past the decimal point, if necessary.

1. A golf tournament with the following final day scores: 86, 88, 68, 74, 72, 75, 74, 80, 70, 82, 67.

   Median = _____   Mode = _____   Mean = _____

2. The weights of vehicles in a quality comparison test: 2,280; 2,375; 2,925.

   Median = _____   Mode = _____   Mean = _____

3. The scores on a spelling test: 70, 80, 90, 100, 90, 100, 70, 80, 100, 60.

   Median = _____   Mode = _____   Mean = _____

4. The cost of the same can of tomatoes priced at different supermarkets:
   $1.25, $1.29, $1.78, $1.06.

   Median = _____   Mode = _____   Mean = _____

5. The high temperatures recorded during one hot summer week: 98, 92, 94, 97, 92, 95, 99.

   Median = _____   Mode = _____   Mean = _____

Name: _____   Date: _____

Section 16 Studying Data

Find the median, mode, and mean for each data set. Round answers off to four places past the decimal point, if necessary.

1. Scores for the day from a round of golf: 87, 89, 65, 75, 70, 74, 75, 81, 72, 83, 68.

   Median = _____   Mode = _____   Mean = _____

2. Shock compression test scores: 2,500; 2,300; 2,800.

   Median = _____   Mode = _____   Mean = _____

3. Science test scores: 75, 85, 95, 100, 95, 100, 75, 85, 100, 65.

   Median = _____   Mode = _____   Mean = _____

4. The cost of the same frozen pot pie priced at different supermarkets: $1.35, $1.30, $1.75, $1.05.

   Median = _____   Mode = _____   Mean = _____

5. The high temperatures recorded during one week in a greenhouse: 98, 99, 95, 96, 93, 95, 99.

   Median = _____

   Mode = _____

   Mean = _____

Name: _____ Date: _____

Section (17) Word Problem Workshop

APPLY   Solve the following mixed-operation word problems. Use a calculator if needed.

1. A poll of 1,200 people found that five-sixths of these people would not buy cherry-flavored ice cream. The rest of the people state they probably would buy ice cream made with cherries. How many people said they probably would buy cherry ice cream?

   _____

2. Nick is a college math student who runs a grass-cutting and lawn-cleanup service. He has observed that it takes 30 minutes to cut a one-fourth-acre-sized lawn. Since customers are charged $20 an hour for work performed, how much should he charge for cutting a one-acre lot?

   _____

3. Serena wants to spread grass seed over her lawn, which is currently in very poor condition. The lawn is rectangular in shape with a width of 40 feet and a length twice the width. One bag of grass seed is enough to cover 40 square feet. How many bags of grass seed will she need for this lawn?

   _____

4. A carpenter has just finished making a large wooden box for holding materials to be recycled. How many cubic feet of material will the box hold if its measurements are 3 feet tall, 4 feet wide, and 4 feet long?

   _____

5. If a water sprinkler sprays a circular pattern with a radius of 20 feet, how much area is the sprinkler capable of covering?

   _____

6. Four large tanks at a factory hold a chemical used for manufacturing. The tanks all have 200-gallon capacities and began the workday at full capacity. Tank 1 is now one-fourth full, Tank 2 is empty, Tank 3 is three-fifths full, and Tank 4 is one-tenth full. How many gallons of the chemical have been used?

   _____

Name: _____ Date: _____

Section 17 Word Problem Workshop

EXTRA PRACTICE Solve the following mixed-operation word problems. Use a calculator if needed.

1. A group of 1,500 people was asked if they would buy a tablet computer in the next year. Three-fourths of the group said no. How many of the group will buy a tablet computer in the next year?

    _____

2. It takes a lawn crew 25 minutes to cut a one-fourth-acre lawn. They charge $30 an hour to work. What would be the cost to cut a 10-acre lot?

    _____

3. James wants to lay sod on his yard. The yard is 50 feet wide by 100 feet long. It costs $1.50 per square foot for sod. How much will it cost to lay sod on his yard?

    _____

4. The local swim club is looking forward to competing in their new Olympic-size swimming pool, which measures 50 meters long by 25 meters wide by 2 meters deep. How many cubic meters of water does this pool hold?

    _____

5. How much area will be covered by a hose with a circular spray pattern with a radius of 15 feet?

    _____

6. A gas station has five tanks of fuel. Each tank contains 500 gallons of fuel. The day started with all tanks full. The first tank is now one-tenth full, the second is three-fourths full, the third tank is full, the fourth is five-eighths full, and the fifth is seven-ninths full. How much fuel has been used?

    _____

7. Rachel wants to build a pen for her new puppy. The area she wants to enclose is eight feet wide by 20 feet long. How much fencing will she have to buy to go around this space?

    _____

Final Review   Covering All Sections

APPLY   List all factors for each number. Write "prime" if the number has only 1 and itself as factors.

1. 24 _____

2. 33 _____

3. 41 _____

Add or subtract as indicated. Reduce answers to lowest terms.

4. $\frac{5}{8} + \frac{1}{8} =$ _____   **5.** $8 - \frac{1}{3} =$ _____

6. $\frac{3}{8} - \frac{2}{9} =$ _____   **7.** $\frac{9}{5} + \frac{2}{5} =$ _____

8. $5\frac{1}{6} - 3\frac{3}{8} =$ _____   **9.** $8\frac{7}{8} + 2\frac{4}{5} =$ _____

10. $1\frac{1}{3} + 2\frac{5}{8} + 7\frac{5}{6} =$ _____

Multiply or divide as indicated. Reduce answers to lowest terms.

11. $\frac{4}{5} \times \frac{3}{4} =$ _____   **12.** $\frac{2}{16} \div \frac{1}{8} =$ _____

13. $4 \times \frac{2}{7} =$ _____   **14.** $\frac{1}{4} \div 5 =$ _____

15. $6 \div \frac{2}{3} =$ _____   **16.** $2\frac{1}{6} \div 1\frac{7}{8} =$ _____

17. $\frac{3}{4} \times \left(1\frac{1}{4} \times \frac{3}{4}\right) =$ _____   **18.** $\left(\frac{2}{3} \times \frac{2}{3}\right) \div \frac{1}{2} =$ _____

Add or subtract as indicated. Reduce answers to lowest terms.

19. $3 + -4 =$ _____   **20.** $6 + -6 =$ _____

21. $-10 + 16 =$ _____   **22.** $0 - 8 =$ _____

23. $-32 + -21 =$ _____   **24.** $-50 - -17 =$ _____

25. $3 + -\frac{1}{2} =$ _____   **26.** $5\frac{1}{4} - -\frac{3}{4} =$ _____

Name: _____ Date: _____

Final Review Covering All Sections

Multiply or divide as indicated. Reduce answers to lowest terms.

27. $3 \times -6 =$ _____

28. $-4 \times -5 =$ _____

29. $25 \times -2 =$ _____

30. $-6 \div -6 =$ _____

31. $-\frac{5}{8} \div 6 =$ _____

32. $4\frac{2}{3} \times -\frac{3}{6} =$ _____

33. $-2 \times \left(-3 \times \frac{1}{6}\right) =$ _____

Solve the expressions using order of operation rules. Reduce answers to lowest terms.

34. $7 \times 8 + 3 =$ _____

35. $80 \div 4 + 6 =$ _____

36. $50 - (50 \div 2) =$ _____

37. $\frac{3}{4} \times \left(\frac{3}{4} + \frac{3}{4}\right) =$ _____

38. $[(15 \times 12) - (20 \div 2) + 82] =$ _____

39. $112 \times [(50 \div 4) - 44] =$ _____

40. $240 - \left[(48 \times 4) + \left(24 \div \frac{1}{2}\right)\right] =$ _____

Determine the square roots of the following numbers.

41. 16 _____

42. 1 _____

43. 400 _____

44. 10,000 _____

Rewrite each expression as a base number with exponent.

45. $6 \times 6 \times 6 \times 6 =$ _____

46. $2 \times 2 \times 2 \times 2 \times 2 \times 2 \times 2 \times 2 =$ _____

47. $25 \times 25 \times 25 =$ _____

Write the numerical equivalent.

48. $2^4 =$ _____

49. $5^3 =$ _____

50. $13^2 =$ _____

51. $10^4 =$ _____

Name: _____ Date: _____

Final Review Covering All Sections

Evaluate the expressions with the values provided.

52. $c - 20$, $c = 51$ _____

53. $40 + t$, $t = -16$ _____

54. $g - 2$, $g = -3$ _____

55. $12 - r$, $r = -24$ _____

Solve for the value of the variable in each equation.

56. $12 - a = 3$, $a =$ _____

57. $r - 10 = 13$, $r =$ _____

58. $y - 8 = 8$, $y =$ _____

59. $h + 7 = 0$, $h =$ _____

60. $3 + 2 + g - 5 = 20$, $g =$ _____

61. $r + 5 = 90 - 65$, $r =$ _____

Simplify the expressions by combining like terms.

62. $k - 50 + 2k - k + 15 + 4k$ _____

63. $14f - 3f + 12f + 16 + 7f - 11 + 13$ _____

64. $20r + 20 - 80r + 40 - 20 + 40r - 20$ _____

65. $100y + 27 + 55y - 37 + 13 - 23y - 41$ _____

Find the perimeter for the figure described.

66. a rectangle with sides 12 inches by 60 inches   Perimeter = _____

67. a square with sides of 4.5 centimeters   Perimeter = _____

68. a regular hexagon with sides of 6 inches   Perimeter = _____

Name: _____   Date: _____

Final Review   **Covering All Sections**

Mixed area and volume practice. Express answers only to four places past the decimal point and round off, where applicable.

69. Find the area of a rectangle with sides of 20 centimeters by 40 centimeters.

Area = _____

70. Find the volume of cube with sides of 6 inches.   Volume = _____

71. Find the area of a circle with a radius of 20 feet.   Area = _____

72. Find the area of a circle with a radius of 12 inches. Area = _____

Find the median, mode, and mean for each data set. Express answers only to four places past the decimal point and round off, where applicable.

73.   50, 60, 55, 65, 90, 40, 50, 80, 105

median = _____

mode = _____

mean = _____

74.   1,020; 1,040; 980; 880; 1,000

median = _____

mode = _____

mean = _____

Name: _____ Date: _____

Final Review Covering All Sections

EXTRA PRACTICE List all factors for each number. Write "prime" if the number has only 1 and itself as factors.

1. 25 _____

2. 32 _____

Add, subtract, multiply, or divide as indicated. Reduce answers to lowest terms.

3. $\frac{3}{8} + \frac{2}{8} =$ _____

4. $9 - \frac{1}{4} =$ _____

5. $\frac{3}{4} - \frac{2}{5} =$ _____

6. $\frac{10}{5} + \frac{3}{5} =$ _____

7. $\frac{3}{4} \times \frac{2}{5} =$ _____

8. $\frac{2}{8} \div \frac{1}{4} =$ _____

9. $5 \times \frac{3}{7} =$ _____

10. $\frac{1}{3} \div 6 =$ _____

Add, subtract, multiply, or divide as indicated. Reduce answers to lowest terms.

11. $2 + -3 =$ _____

12. $4 + -4 =$ _____

13. $-12 + 15 =$ _____

14. $0 - 9 =$ _____

15. $4 \times -5 =$ _____

16. $-6 \times -4 =$ _____

17. $26 \times -3 =$ _____

18. $-5 \div -5 =$ _____

19. $\frac{9}{12} \div 4 =$ _____

20. $2\frac{5}{8} \times -\frac{2}{3} =$ _____

Solve the expressions using order of operation rules. Reduce answers to lowest terms.

21. $7 \times 9 + 4 =$ _____

22. $90 \div 6 + 2 =$ _____

23. $40 - (40 \div 3) =$ _____

24. $\frac{1}{2} \times \left(\frac{3}{4} + \frac{5}{6}\right) =$ _____

Determine the square roots of the following numbers.

25. 36 _____

26. 2 _____

Name: _____   Date: _____

Final Review **Covering All Sections**

Rewrite each expression as a base number with exponent.

27. 5 x 5 x 5 x 5 x 5 = _____

28. 3 x 3 x 3 x 3 x 3 x 3 x 3 x 3 x 3 = _____

Write the numerical equivalent.

29. 3^5 = _____   **30.** 6^2 = _____

Evaluate the expressions with the values provided.

31. $x - 50$, $x = 25$ _____   **32.** $20 + t$, $t = -15$ _____

Solve for the value of the variable in each equation.

33. $15 - a = 4$, $a =$ _____   **34.** $y - 12 = 15$, $y =$ _____

35. $h - 7 = 9$, $h =$ _____   **36.** $m + 9 = -2$, $m =$ _____

Simplify the expressions by combining like terms.

37. $a - 30 + 3a - a + 12 + 5a$ _____

38. $15d - 2d + 13d + 15 + 8d - 10 + 12$ _____

Find the perimeter for the figure described.

39. a rectangle with sides 15 inches by 30 inches   Perimeter = _____

40. a square with sides of 3.2 centimeters   Perimeter = _____

41. a circle with radius of 6.5 centimeters   Circumference = _____

42. a circle with diameter of 12 inches   Circumference = _____

Name: _____ Date: _____

Final Review **Covering All Sections**

Mixed area and volume practice. Express answers only to four places past the decimal point and round off, where applicable.

43. Find the area of a rectangle with sides of 15 centimeters by 20 centimeters.

Area = _____

44. Find the area of a circle with a radius of 9 inches. Area = _____

45. Find the area of a circle with a diameter of 14 centimeters. Area = _____

46. Find the volume of a cube with sides of 5 inches. Volume = _____

47. Find the volume of a rectangular prism with width of 6 cm, height of 5.5 cm, and length of 13 cm.

Volume = _____

Find the median, mode, and mean for each data set. Express answers only to four places past the decimal point and round off, where applicable.

48. 25, 30, 52, 62, 45, 20, 25, 40, 102   **49.** 203, 210, 205, 205

median = _____   median = _____

mode = _____   mode = _____

mean = _____   mean = _____

50. 17, 25, 23, 18, 19, 15, 22, 23, 18, 21

median = _____

mode = _____

mean = _____

Answer Keys

Section 1: Factoring Numbers
Apply (p. 3)
1. 1, 2, 4
2. 1, 2, 3, 4, 6, 12
3. 1, 2, 3, 6, 9, 18
4. prime
5. 1, 2, 3, 4, 6, 8, 12, 16, 24, 48
6. 1, 5, 11, 55
7. prime
8. prime
9. 1, 2, 3, 5, 6, 9, 10, 15, 18, 30, 45, 90
10. 1, 3, 5, 7, 15, 21, 35, 105
11. 1, 3, 37, 111
12. 1, 2, 4, 5, 8, 10, 20, 25, 40, 50, 100, 200
13. 1, 7, 43, 301
14. 1, 2, 4, 5, 8, 10, 16, 20, 25, 40, 50, 80, 100, 200, 400
15. 1, 5, 17, 25, 85, 425

Extra Practice (p. 4)
1. prime
2. 1, 2, 7, 14
3. prime
4. 1, 2, 4, 8, 16, 32
5. 1, 7, 49
6. 1, 2, 5, 10, 25, 50
7. 1, 2, 4, 17, 34, 68
8. 1, 2, 3, 4, 6, 8, 9, 12, 18, 24, 36, 72
9. 1, 3, 9, 11, 33, 99
10. 1, 2, 5, 10, 11, 22, 55, 110
11. 1, 5, 25, 125
12. 1, 2, 5, 10, 25, 50, 125, 250
13. 1, 5, 61, 305
14. 1, 5, 83, 415
15. 1, 2, 3, 5, 6, 9, 10, 15, 18, 25, 30, 45, 50, 75, 90, 150, 225, 450
16. 1, 2, 4, 5, 10, 20, 25, 50, 100, 125, 250, 500
17. 1, 5, 23, 25, 115, 575
18. 1, 5, 11, 55, 121, 605
19. 1, 2, 4, 5, 10, 20, 31, 62, 124, 155, 310, 620
20. 1, 2, 3, 6, 9, 13, 18, 26, 27, 39, 54, 78, 117, 234, 351, 702

Section 2: Adding and Subtracting Fractions
Apply: Quick Review (p. 5)
1. $\frac{3}{5}$
2. $\frac{1}{11}$
3. $\frac{1}{5}$
4. $\frac{1}{25}$
5. $\frac{1}{4}$
6. $\frac{5}{6}$

Extra Practice (p. 6)
1. $\frac{7}{10}$
2. $\frac{1}{11}$
3. $\frac{8}{45}$
4. $\frac{2}{75}$
5. $\frac{1}{3}$
6. $\frac{3}{7}$
7. $\frac{2}{5}$
8. $\frac{1}{12}$
9. $\frac{2}{9}$
10. $\frac{1}{20}$
11. $\frac{1}{7}$
12. $\frac{1}{2}$
13. $\frac{4}{5}$
14. $\frac{1}{11}$
15. $\frac{1}{9}$
16. $\frac{1}{30}$
17. $\frac{1}{7}$
18. $\frac{8}{9}$
19. $\frac{9}{10}$
20. $\frac{1}{10}$

Apply (p. 7)
1. $\frac{5}{7}$
2. $\frac{3}{4}$
3. $\frac{13}{24}$
4. $\frac{7}{12}$
5. $1\frac{16}{45}$
6. $\frac{7}{10}$
7. $\frac{20}{81}$
8. $\frac{7}{15}$
9. $2\frac{1}{5}$
10. $2\frac{1}{4}$
11. $\frac{1}{11}$
12. 1

13. $3\frac{11}{12}$ **14.** $2\frac{1}{3}$ **15.** $5\frac{6}{11}$ **16.** $1\frac{1}{3}$ **17.** $2\frac{11}{12}$ **18.** $1\frac{7}{8}$

19. $4\frac{5}{8}$ **20.** 1 **21.** $1\frac{9}{16}$ **22.** 8 **23.** $2\frac{2}{15}$ **24.** $7\frac{1}{2}$

25. 3

Extra Practice (p. 8)

1. $1\frac{1}{7}$ **2.** $\frac{7}{8}$ **3.** $\frac{1}{12}$ **4.** $\frac{5}{12}$ **5.** $1\frac{4}{15}$ **6.** $\frac{17}{20}$

7. $\frac{44}{81}$ **8.** $\frac{28}{45}$ **9.** $3\frac{6}{35}$ **10.** $2\frac{1}{8}$ **11.** $\frac{1}{11}$ **12.** $2\frac{1}{2}$

13. $3\frac{3}{4}$ **14.** $2\frac{8}{9}$ **15.** $2\frac{27}{44}$ **16.** 1 **17.** $2\frac{5}{6}$ **18.** 1

19. $6\frac{3}{4}$ **20.** $1\frac{3}{10}$ **21.** $1\frac{25}{28}$ **22.** 6

Section 3: Multiplying and Dividing Fractions
Apply: Quick Review (p. 10)

1. $\frac{27}{8}$ **2.** $\frac{37}{8}$ **3.** $\frac{71}{9}$ **4.** $\frac{13}{12}$ **5.** $\frac{11}{1}$ **6.** $\frac{34}{15}$

Apply (p. 10)

1. $\frac{1}{20}$ **2.** $\frac{2}{7}$ **3.** $\frac{2}{15}$ **4.** $\frac{1}{2}$ **5.** $2\frac{2}{3}$ **6.** $\frac{4}{15}$

7. $\frac{3}{4}$ **8.** 5 **9.** 8 **10.** $\frac{3}{8}$ **11.** $6\frac{2}{3}$ **12.** $4\frac{1}{2}$

13. $\frac{26}{27}$ **14.** $4\frac{23}{24}$ **15.** $\frac{1}{2}$ **16.** 34 **17.** $2\frac{4}{7}$ **18.** $1\frac{3}{10}$

19. $1\frac{1}{9}$ **20.** $3\frac{3}{4}$

Extra Practice (p. 11)
Mixed Numbers to Improper Fractions

1. $\frac{18}{5}$ **2.** $\frac{56}{10}$ **3.** $\frac{61}{9}$ **4.** $\frac{16}{12}$ **5.** $\frac{13}{1}$ **6.** $\frac{36}{15}$

7. $\frac{37}{8}$ **8.** $\frac{47}{4}$ **9.** $\frac{19}{2}$ **10.** $\frac{17}{7}$ **11.** $\frac{20}{1}$ **12.** $\frac{32}{3}$

Improper Fractions to Mixed Numbers

1. $3\frac{2}{5}$ **2.** 9 **3.** $2\frac{1}{2}$ **4.** $3\frac{1}{12}$ **5.** 42 **6.** $4\frac{13}{17}$

7. $4\frac{4}{5}$ **8.** $5\frac{1}{5}$ **9.** 8 **10.** $9\frac{2}{3}$ **11.** $3\frac{2}{3}$ **12.** $4\frac{1}{2}$

Extra Practice (p. 12)

1. $\frac{2}{15}$ **2.** $\frac{3}{7}$ **3.** $\frac{14}{45}$ **4.** $1\frac{2}{3}$ **5.** $1\frac{5}{16}$ **6.** $\frac{4}{15}$

7. $3\frac{3}{4}$ **8.** $6\frac{3}{7}$ **9.** 6 **10.** $\frac{3}{8}$ **11.** $22\frac{1}{2}$ **12.** $15\frac{3}{4}$

13. $\frac{5}{21}$ **14.** $10\frac{1}{3}$ **15.** $\frac{8}{15}$ **16.** $2\frac{5}{6}$ **17.** $1\frac{8}{217}$ **18.** $1\frac{3}{10}$

19. $1\frac{1}{4}$ **20.** $\frac{9}{14}$ **21.** $2\frac{1}{8}$ **22.** $5\frac{5}{7}$ **23.** $3\frac{11}{15}$ **24.** $1\frac{4}{5}$

Section 4: Positive and Negative Numbers
Apply (p. 14)

1. -2	**2.** 6	**3.** -7	**4.** -9	**5.** -10	**6.** 2
7. -16	**8.** -3	**9.** 98	**10.** 70	**11.** -14	**12.** 7
13. 24	**14.** -56	**15.** -10	**16.** -20	**17.** 700	**18.** -25
19. $1\frac{3}{4}$	**20.** $\frac{1}{2}$	**21.** 7	**22.** -1	**23.** $12\frac{3}{4}$	**24.** 0
25. $-\frac{9}{20}$					

Extra Practice (p. 15)

1. -2	**2.** 10	**3.** -8	**4.** -10	**5.** 2	**6.** 5
7. -12	**8.** -1	**9.** 195	**10.** 60	**11.** -50	**12.** 18
13. 50	**14.** -77	**15.** -4	**16.** -20	**17.** 1,000	**18.** 50
19. $2\frac{2}{3}$	**20.** $\frac{1}{5}$	**21.** $\frac{5}{8}$	**22.** $-5\frac{3}{10}$	**23.** $-1\frac{4}{9}$	**24.** $-\frac{7}{10}$
25. $-14\frac{7}{15}$					

Section 5: Multiplying and Dividing With Negative Numbers
Apply (p. 16–17)

1. -72	**2.** -1	**3.** 9	**4.** 0	**5.** -90	**6.** -2
7. -9	**8.** -3	**9.** 144	**10.** -10	**11.** 1	**12.** -44
13. 10	**14.** -24	**15.** 100	**16.** -500	**17.** 400	**18.** 0
19. 60	**20.** -400	**21.** $\frac{3}{16}$	**22.** -4	**23.** $-\frac{1}{12}$	**24.** -16
25. -3	**26.** -1	**27.** 10	**28.** $-1\frac{1}{4}$	**29.** $-\frac{3}{16}$	**30.** $4\frac{23}{24}$

Extra Practice (p. 18)

1. -20	**2.** -2.5	**3.** 576	**4.** -10	**5.** 1	**6.** -66
7. 10	**8.** -12	**9.** 180	**10.** -750	**11.** 900	**12.** 0
13. 480	**14.** -1,000	**15.** $\frac{3}{25}$	**16.** $-5\frac{1}{4}$	**17.** $-\frac{1}{15}$	**18.** -25
19. -9	**20.** -1	**21.** $-\frac{3}{5}$	**22.** $-\frac{8}{33}$	**23.** $5\frac{1}{3}$	**24.** $-\frac{6}{7}$

Section 6: Order of Operations
Apply (p. 20)

1. 51	**2.** 8	**3.** 12	**4.** 33	**5.** 6	**6.** 22
7. 5	**8.** 32	**9.** 50	**10.** 12	**11.** -4	**12.** -30
13. $2\frac{2}{3}$	**14.** -120	**15.** -190	**16.** 100	**17.** $3\frac{1}{48}$	**18.** 53
19. $-5\frac{13}{36}$	**20.** 426	**21.** 11	**22.** 938		

Extra Practice (p. 21)

1. 70	**2.** 0	**3.** 10	**4.** 36	**5.** 6.5	**6.** 25
7. 5	**8.** 88	**9.** 100	**10.** 12	**11.** -6	**12.** -30
13. $1\frac{3}{5}$	**14.** -5	**15.** $-433\frac{1}{3}$	**16.** $2\frac{11}{16}$	**17.** 115	**18.** -123
19. 2,540	**20.** 178				

Section Review 1: Covering Sections 1 Through 6
Apply (p. 22–23)

1. 1, 2, 3, 4, 6, 9, 12, 18, 36   **2.** prime

3. 1, 2, 4, 7, 8, 14, 28, 56   **4.** 1, 2, 3, 4, 5, 6, 10, 12, 15, 20, 30, 60

5. $1\frac{5}{9}$ **6.** $\frac{3}{28}$ **7.** $2\frac{1}{5}$ **8.** $4\frac{3}{8}$ **9.** $7\frac{1}{2}$ **10.** $\frac{3}{88}$

11. $10\frac{7}{40}$ **12.** $\frac{1}{18}$ **13.** $2\frac{2}{7}$ **14.** $\frac{3}{32}$ **15.** $6\frac{1}{5}$ **16.** 24

17. $13\frac{1}{8}$ **18.** $1\frac{3}{10}$ **19.** -1   **20.** 13   **21.** -27   **22.** -10

23. -4   **24.** -8   **25.** 0   **26.** 450   **27.** 288   **28.** 59

29. 0   **30.** 19   **31.** 18   **32.** 24   **33.** 19   **34.** 56

35. 1,448   **36.** -8   **37.** $65.40   **38.** $375.00   **39.** 150   **40.** 8,200

Extra Practice (p. 24–25)

1. 1, 2, 3, 4, 6, 8, 12, 16, 24, 48   **2.** 1, 2, 5, 10, 25, 50

3. prime   **4.** 1, 2, 7, 14, 49, 98

5. $2\frac{2}{3}$ **6.** $\frac{1}{20}$ **7.** $4\frac{2}{15}$ **8.** $4\frac{11}{36}$ **9.** $6\frac{1}{2}$ **10.** $1\frac{17}{35}$

11. $\frac{4}{5}$ **12.** $\frac{4}{5}$ **13.** $\frac{5}{48}$ **14.** $2\frac{1}{2}$ **15.** $\frac{3}{16}$ **16.** 3

17. $3\frac{13}{15}$ **18.** 21   **19.** $\frac{21}{32}$ **20.** $3\frac{1}{3}$ **21.** -3   **22.** 25

23. -6   **24.** -7   **25.** 148   **26.** -6   **27.** 17   **28.** -5

29. $-\frac{12}{25}$ **30.** $-26\frac{2}{3}$ **31.** $2\frac{1}{4}$ **32.** $1\frac{9}{20}$ **33.** $-4\frac{1}{10}$ **34.** $\frac{2}{7}$

35. 188   **36.** 68   **37.** -$53.25   **38.** $525   **39.** 80   **40.** 9

Section 7: Squares and Square Roots
Apply (p. 27)

1. 25   **2.** 16   **3.** 121   **4.** 4   **5.** 256   **6.** 400

7. 1   **8.** 11.56   **9.** 77.44   **10.** $\frac{1}{16}$ **11.** $6\frac{1}{4}$ **12.** $\frac{49}{64}$

13. 8   **14.** 6   **15.** 9   **16.** 8.3666   **17.** 11.1803   **18.** 14.8324

19. 30   **20.** 34.6410

Extra Practice (p. 28)

1. 64   **2.** 36   **3.** 144   **4.** 9   **5.** 225   **6.** 900

7. 20.25   **8.** 43.56   **9.** $\frac{1}{9}$ **10.** $10\frac{9}{16}$ **11.** 7.8740   **12.** 4.8990

13. 7   **14.** 9.3808   **15.** 11.0454   **16.** 6   **17.** 10   **18.** 20.6882

19. 35   **20.** 61.7819

Section 8: Exponents
Apply (p. 30)
1. 64	**2.** 256	**3.** 729	**4.** 1,728	**5.** 2,500	**6.** 16,807
7. 256	**8.** 3,375	**9.** 25^5	**10.** 10^5	**11.** 4^7	**12.** 120^3
13. 3^3	**14.** 2^5	**15.** 5^3	**16.** 10^3		

Extra Practice (p. 31)
1. 243	**2.** 27	**3.** 6,561	**4.** 50,625	**5.** 625	**6.** 512
7. 537,824	**8.** 324	**9.** 50^4	**10.** 12^3	**11.** 2^7	**12.** 100^5
13. 5^2	**14.** 6^2	**15.** 12^3	**16.** 10^4 or 100^2		

Section 9: What Is a Variable
Apply (p. 32)
Answers will vary.

Section 10: Expressions With Variables
Apply (p. 34)
1. 22	**2.** 6	**3.** 33	**4.** 64	**5.** -14	**6.** 0
7. 1	**8.** $1\frac{3}{4}$	**9.** 22	**10.** 19	**11.** 9	**12.** 12
13. 32	**14.** 21	**15.** 36	**16.** -14	**17.** -1	**18.** -8
19. 0	**20.** $1\frac{1}{2}$	**21.** $\frac{2}{3}$	**22.** 5		

Extra Practice (p. 35)
1. 13	**2.** 5	**3.** 35	**4.** 80	**5.** -40	**6.** -10
7. 1	**8.** $-\frac{3}{4}$	**9.** 23	**10.** 27	**11.** 10	**12.** 13
13. 30	**14.** 23	**15.** 37	**16.** -13	**17.** 1	**18.** -4
19. 0	**20.** $3\frac{3}{4}$	**21.** $6\frac{2}{3}$	**22.** 5		

Section 11: More Practice With Variables
Apply (p. 37)
1. $3k + 3$	**2.** $3y - 14$	**3.** 7	**4.** $4c - 16$
5. 70	**6.** 0	**7.** $-19n - 20$	**8.** $72f$
9. $-8t + 220$ or $220 - 8t$	**10.** $96r - 32$ or $-32 + 96r$		**11.** $y - 12$; -9
12. $2t + 2\frac{1}{4}$; $3\frac{1}{4}$	**13.** $-4y + 138$ or $138 - 4y$; 130		**14.** $20w - 106$; -46
15. $5k - 20$; -10			

Extra Practice (p. 38)
1. $3x + 5$	**2.** $5y - 14$	**3.** $z + 3$	**4.** $6d - 15$
5. $-3k + 75$ or $75 - 3k$	**6.** 4	**7.** $-18n + 50$ or $50 - 18n$	**8.** $112f$
9. $-10r + 280$ or $280 - 10r$	**10.** $97g - 25$ or $-25 + 97g$	**11.** $6a - 1$	
12. $30 + 44s$	**13.** $14 + 17n$	**14.** $18q + 75$	**15.** $11d + 22$

Extra Practice (p. 39)

1. $3q - 11$; 4   2. $3f + 2\frac{1}{2}$; 7   3. $160 - 5d$; 145   4. $16w - 119$; 41

5. $7v - 30$; 19   6. $-2w - 4$; -34   7. $-3z + 5\frac{3}{4}$; $-18\frac{1}{4}$ 8. $241 - 9t$; 178

9. $26h - 93$; 167   10. $8m - 38$; 154

Section Review 2: Covering Sections 1 Through 11
Apply (p. 40–42)

1. 1, 2, 3, 6   2. 1, 3, 7, 21   3. 1, 2, 4, 5, 8, 10, 20, 40

4. 1, 3, 17, 51   5. 1, 2, 37, 74   6. 1, 2, 4, 8, 16, 32, 64, 128

7. 1, 2, 5, 10, 25, 50, 125, 250

8. $1\frac{1}{4}$ 9. $\frac{3}{4}$ 10. $1\frac{4}{9}$ 11. $1\frac{47}{72}$ 12. $3\frac{25}{36}$ 13. $4\frac{2}{5}$

14. 3   15. $1\frac{7}{12}$ 16. $\frac{9}{16}$ 17. $\frac{2}{5}$ 18. 32   19. $3\frac{9}{32}$

20. $10\frac{3}{4}$ 21. $66\frac{2}{3}$ 22. $3\frac{3}{5}$ 23. 0   24. -6   25. -12

26. -10   27. 0   28. -12   29. 14   30. 7   31. $\frac{3}{4}$

32. $-4\frac{3}{4}$ 33. -60   34. -36   35. 90   36. -1   37. $-\frac{9}{16}$

38. -10   39. -48   40. $1\frac{1}{7}$ 41. 16   42. 40   43. 100

44. 98   45. 180   46. 58   47. 4.8990   48. 8   49. 9.1652

50. 8.4261   51. 16   52. 216   53. 30^5 54. 12^4 55. 6^7

56. 8   57. 2   58. -1   59. -18   60. 0   61. 13

62. -4   63. 40   64. $4r + 4$ 65. $4h + 19$ 66. $20y + 50$

Extra Practice (p. 43–44)

1. prime   2. 1, 2, 11, 22

3. 1, 5, 7, 35   4. 1, 2, 5, 10, 25, 50

5. 1   6. $\frac{17}{30}$ 7. $\frac{8}{9}$ 8. $1\frac{7}{24}$ 9. $\frac{25}{81}$ 10. $\frac{9}{10}$

11. 45   12. $1\frac{13}{32}$ 13. 0   14. -6   15. -15   16. -9

17. 0   18. -50   19. -64   20. 40   21. -1   22. 12

23. 50   24. 1,000   25. 5   26. 7.7460   27. 10.2470   28. 9

29. 25   30. 64   31. 2,401   32. 16,384   33. 20^5 34. 15^3

35. 2^8 36. 40^2 37. 10   38. 0   39. 22   40. 46

41. 3   42. 47   43. -11   44. 11   45. $5a + 6$ 46. $6f + 27$

47. $10 + 7s$ 48. $16y + 17$

Section 12: Perimeter and Area
Apply (p. 46–47)

1. 24 in.   2. 25 cm   3. 16 ft.   4. 20 sq. cm   5. $6\frac{1}{4}$ sq. in.   6. 21 sq. cm

Extra Practice: Perimeter (p. 48)
1. 48 in.   2. 40 cm   3. 50 ft.   4. 34 in.   5. 24 ft.

Extra Practice: Area (p. 49)
1. 24 cm²   2. 20.25 in.²   3. 50 cm²   4. 49 ft.²   5. 54 in.²

Section 13: Volume
Apply (p. 51)
1. 192 cu. in.   2. 125 cu. cm   3. 320,000 cu. ft.
4. 8,640 cu. ft.   5. 20,736 cu. in. or 12 cu. ft.   6. 13,728 cu. cm

Extra Practice (p. 52)
1. 288 in.³   2. 512 cm³   3. 3,750 ft.³
4. 10,125 ft.³   5. 3,456 in.³ or 2 ft.³   6. 11,250 cm³

Section 14: Working With Circles
Apply (p. 54–55)
1. C = 43.981 in.   A = 153.9335 in.²   2. C = 15.7075 ft.   A = 19.6344 ft.²
3. C = 276.452 cm   A = 6,081.944 cm²   4. C = 21.9905 in.   A = 38.4834 in.²
5. C = 18.849 ft.   A = 28.2735 ft.²   6. C = 157.075 cm   A = 1,963.4375 cm²
7. C = 4.7123 in.   A = 1.7671 in.²

Extra Practice (p. 56)
1. C = 37.698 in.   A = 113.094 in.²   2. C = 21.9905 ft.   A = 38.4834 ft.²
3. C = 282.735 cm   A = 6,361.5375 cm²   4. C = 25.132 in.   A = 50.264 in.²
5. C = 25.132 ft.   A = 50.264 ft.²   6. C = 141.3675 cm   A = 1,590.3843 cm²
7. C = 7.8538 in.   A = 4.9086 in.²   8. C = 22.6188 cm   A = 40.7138 cm²

Section 15: Basic Properties of Numbers
Apply (p. 57)
1. no   2. yes   3. yes   4. yes   5. no   6. yes
7. yes   8. no   9. yes   10. yes

Extra Practice (p. 58)
1. no   2. no   3. no   4. yes   5. no   6. yes
7. yes   8. no   9. yes   10. yes   11. associative
12. commutative   13. associative   14. distributive
15. commutative

Section 16: Studying Data
Apply (p. 60)
Listed in the following order: median, mode, mean
1. 74, 74, 76   2. 2,375; none; 2,526.6667   3. 85, 100, 84
4. $1.27, none, $1.35   5. 95, 92, 95.2857

Extra Practice (p. 61)
Listed in the following order: median, mode, mean
1. 75, 75, 76.2227   2. 2,500; none; 2,533.3333   3. 90, 100, 87.5
4. $1.33, no, $1.36   5. 96, 95 & 99, 96.4286

Section 17: Word Problem Workshop
Apply (p. 62)
1. 200 people
2. $40
3. 80 bags
4. 48 cu. ft.
5. 1,256.60 sq. ft.
6. 610 gallons

Extra Practice (p. 63)
1. 375 people
2. $500
3. $7,500
4. 2,500 cu. m
5. 706.8375 sq. ft.
6. 873.6 gallons
7. 56 ft.

Final Review: Covering All Sections
Apply (p. 64–67)
1. 1, 2, 3, 4, 6, 8, 12, 24
2. 1, 3, 11, 33
3. prime
4. $\frac{3}{4}$
5. $7\frac{2}{3}$
6. $\frac{11}{72}$
7. $2\frac{1}{5}$
8. $1\frac{19}{24}$
9. $11\frac{27}{40}$
10. $11\frac{19}{24}$
11. $\frac{3}{5}$
12. 1
13. $1\frac{1}{7}$
14. $\frac{1}{20}$
15. 9
16. $1\frac{7}{45}$
17. $\frac{45}{64}$
18. $\frac{8}{9}$
19. -1
20. 0
21. 6
22. -8
23. -53
24. -33
25. $2\frac{1}{2}$
26. 6
27. -18
28. 20
29. -50
30. 1
31. $-\frac{5}{48}$
32. $-2\frac{1}{3}$
33. 1
34. 59
35. 26
36. 25
37. $1\frac{1}{8}$
38. 252
39. -3,528
40. 0
41. 4
42. 1
43. 20
44. 100
45. 6^4
46. 2^8
47. 25^3
48. 16
49. 125
50. 169
51. 10,000
52. 31
53. 24
54. -5
55. 36
56. 9
57. 23
58. 16
59. -7
60. 20
61. 20
62. $6k - 35$
63. $30f + 18$
64. $-20r + 20$
65. $132y - 38$
66. 144 in.
67. 18 cm
68. 36 in.
69. 800 cm^2
70. 216 in.^{3}
71. 1,256.6 ft.^{2}
72. 452.376 in.^{2}
73. median 60, mode 50, mean 66.1111
74. median 1,000; mode none; mean 984

Extra Practice (p. 68–70)
1. 1, 5, 25
2. 1, 2, 4, 8, 16, 32
3. $\frac{5}{8}$
4. $8\frac{3}{4}$
5. $\frac{7}{20}$
6. $2\frac{3}{5}$
7. $\frac{3}{10}$
8. 1
9. $2\frac{1}{7}$
10. $\frac{1}{18}$
11. -1
12. 0
13. 3
14. -9
15. -20
16. 24
17. -78
18. 1
19. $\frac{3}{16}$
20. $-1\frac{3}{4}$
21. 67
22. 17
23. 26.7
24. $\frac{19}{24}$
25. 6
26. 1.4142
27. 5^5
28. 3^9
29. 243
30. 36
31. -25
32. 5
33. 11
34. 27
35. 16
36. -11
37. $8a - 18$
38. $34d + 17$
39. 90 in.
40. 12.8 cm
41. 40.8395 cm
42. 37.698 in.
43. 300 cm^2
44. 254.4615 in.^{2}
45. 153.9335 cm^2
46. 125 in.^{3}
47. 429 cm^3
48. median 40, mode 25, mean 44.5556
49. median 205, mode 205, mean 205.75
50. median 20, mode 18 & 23, mean 20.1